Drugs in Sport

ISSUES
(formerly Issues for the Nineties)

Volume 26

Editor

Craig Donnellan

Independence
Educational Publishers
Cambridge

First published by Independence
PO Box 295
Cambridge CB1 3XP
England

British Library Cataloguing in Publication Data
Drugs in Sport – (Issues Series)
I. Donnellan, Craig II. Series
362.2'9'088796

ISBN 1 86168 129 1

Printed in Great Britain
The Burlington Press
Cambridge

Typeset by
Claire Boyd

Cover
The illustration on the front cover is by
Pumpkin House.

CONTENTS

Introduction

Drugs in Sport is the twenty-sixth volume in the **Issues** series. The aim of this series is to offer up-to-date information about important issues in our world.

Drugs in Sport looks at drug abuse in sport and drug testing.

The information comes from a wide variety of sources and includes:
Government reports and statistics
Newspaper reports and features
Magazine articles and surveys
Literature from lobby groups
and charitable organisations.

It is hoped that, as you read about the many aspects of the issues explored in this book, you will critically evaluate the information presented. It is important that you decide whether you are being presented with facts or opinions. Does the writer give a biased or an unbiased report? If an opinion is being expressed, do you agree with the writer?

Drugs in Sport offers a useful starting-point for those who need convenient access to information about the many issues involved. However, it is only a starting-point. At the back of the book is a list of organisations which you may want to contact for further information.

*****

The history of drug use in sport

Information from the Australian Sports Drugs Agency

Introduction

The use of drugs in an attempt to enhance sporting performance is often referred to as doping. It is thought that the word 'dope' originated from the South African language. Dope referred to a primitive alcoholic drink that was used as a stimulant in ceremonial dances. Gradually the term adopted a wider usage, and in reference to sport, it became known as 'doping'. In today's sporting context, doping refers to the use by athletes of banned substances or methods that may enhance performance.

While the term doping first appeared in an English dictionary in 1879, the use of drugs is evident throughout the history of sport.

Early games

By 800BC the Greeks had incorporated sport into their lifestyles to a similar extent as the cultural and religious observances of the time. Athletic festivals were common in the Greek calendar. Emphasis was placed on the artistic nature of athletics as well as the preparatory role athletics played for warriors. Participants were required to write poetry, or perhaps display another artistic ability, as well as perform physical feats.

Athletic celebrations of this time were also an important means of establishing the geographic, economic and political importance of an area or region.

From about 400BC, sport achieved a status in the social life of Greece similar to, if not greater than, its place in society today. Mass spectator sport was the order of the day and rich prizes for winners led to the emergence of a class of highly paid sports people, resulting in the demise of the amateur competitor.

Writings from the time of Plato reveal that the value of a victory in the ancient Olympics was the equivalent of nearly half a million dollars. This was complemented by other rewards including food, homes, tax exemptions and even deferment from the armed service.

Professionalism and commercialism ultimately led to corruption. Bribing and cheating became commonplace, and competitors of this period were reputedly willing to ingest any preparation which might enhance their performance, including extracts of mushrooms and plant seeds. In addition to political interference, one of the significant reasons for the dissolution of the ancient Olympic games was the use of drugs.

Roman period

The increased status of sport and the elevated position of athletes continued into the Roman period. However, the Romans adopted different sporting activities to the Greeks.

Spectatorship thrived at gladiatorial competitions and chariot races, and these sporting events reigned as a source of public entertainment. To accommodate the huge following, the Colosseum was restructured in AD100 to hold 60,000 spectators.

The use of drugs during this period has also been recorded. Chariot racers fed their horses a potent mixture to make them run faster, while many gladiators were 'doped-up' to make their fights sufficiently vigorous and bloody for the paying public.

Christian era

The onset of the Christian era signalled the demise of these early games. The blood-letting nature of many of the Roman 'sports' was unacceptable to the new order of society. Eventually in AD396 the Emperor Theodosius called an end to the ancient games with a rule banning all forms of 'pagan' sports.

While sports such as wrestling and boxing were initially promoted as substitutes for the disfavoured Roman activities, these were not widely accepted and their popularity as a form of sport subsided.

Furthermore, the ethos that physical development hindered intellectual development was widely encouraged and accepted.

It was not until the nineteenth century that sport re-emerged. The impetus for this resurgence occurred in rural England and quickly spread throughout the rest of the world.

Sport in the early nineteenth century

Sport in the English society of the early nineteenth century was comprised largely of unstructured recreational activities. England was an agricultural and rural-based society and displayed forms of physical activity that were casual, communal and regionalised in nature. The type of recreational activity mirrored the pace of society.

Celebrations in respect of the harvest, or religious holidays such as Christmas, would bring the village together for a central form of entertainment. Typical celebrations consisted of:

- drinking and dancing
- games such as sack races, leapfrog and pig chasing
- activities like cockfighting and boxing matches
- football games with over 1,000 players on a field several miles long.

The onset of industrialisation and urbanisation transformed the pattern of these rural games.

Sport and the Industrial Revolution

By the latter part of the nineteenth century the rural nature of sport had given way to the influences of

... IN MY DAY YOU WERE CRAZY IF YOU WEREN'T ON DRUGS...

industrialisation and urbanisation. More organised and sophisticated forms of sporting activity emerged.

The reason for changes to traditional forms of sport can be found in wider developments in the structure and organisation of society during this period.

A number of factors influenced society during the Industrial Revolution. Major changes occurred in:

Technology

The invention of new machines and manufacturing processes was the catalyst of industrialisation and urbanisation. The city became the centre of production, and following the mechanisation of many rural activities, people flocked to the cities in the search for employment.

Communication

Greater communication between people and places was required by this more sophisticated society. New forms of communication emerged such as telegraph, penny post, the newspaper and the telephone.

Transportation

Developments in transportation provided better means by which to distribute goods and services to the industrialised society. The emergence of canals, railroads and steamships also aided communication. Prior to the Industrial Revolution, travel was only undertaken for important matters. Improved methods of transportation meant that people were able to travel more freely.

CONTENTS

Lifestyle

People moving to the cities in search of employment had to adapt from the slow-paced regional lifestyle to the quicker, more regimented living required of an urban-based population. The concept of time also became important during this period. Industrialisation brought a clear distinction between work and leisure time.

Political, economic and social structure

These factors influenced lifestyle but also contributed individually to developing the society of this period. New economic and social concerns associated with the industrial society emerged, while the power of government and an emerging middle class were important factors shaping the new society.

Influence on sport

The new urban-based population of the late nineteenth century established restricted, controlled games and activities that reflected the new regulated society. Football games played by thousands of players on a field with no boundaries were not appropriate in the city centres.

A number of developments occurred that changed the format of traditional activities. These included:
- restrictions of time and space
- formation of clubs and organised competitions
- restriction on the number of players
- development of rules

- standardisation and modification of equipment.

As the old forms of activities were modified, new sports such as rugby union, roller skating and ten-pin bowling emerged, while activities like animal baiting and cockfighting lost popularity and were eventually banned.

The Industrial Revolution had a significant impact on all aspects of sport and recreation. Technology was used to develop new equipment in sports such as golf, tennis and cricket. Other inventions also had a major impact, for example, the electric light which permitted the playing of games at night.

Improved communications enabled sports news to be despatched along cable and telephone lines, and developments in transportation allowed for inter-town and eventually international competition. These factors led to increased participation in sporting and recreational activities and significantly contributed to spreading interest in sporting activity world-wide.

Two significant outcomes of the increased involvement and interest

---

During the twentieth century, sporting activity has gradually evolved into a 'big business' providing a significant, world-wide source of entertainment

---

in sport were commercialism and professionalism. Mass spectator sport replaced the communal festival and religious celebrations of earlier times.

Crowds at major soccer matches grew from a few thousand during the middle of the nineteenth century to over 100,000 by the early 1900s. Sporting facilities such as major stadiums were built and sporting events received greater coverage in newspapers and specialist magazines.

Soon the professional sports-person took a place in society. Sport was no longer a frivolous activity to be played solely in free time. Sport, for some, now became a profession.

Sport and the twentieth century

By the turn of the century, sport was reassuming a place similar to that which it held in Greek and Roman societies. Further advances in technology combined with social, economic and political developments influenced sports development during the twentieth century.

During the twentieth century, sporting activity has gradually evolved into a 'big business' providing a significant, world-wide source of entertainment, revenue and employment.

Sport has also developed into a significant social institution and to succeed in sport has become highly valued. This has placed pressure on sports people to become not only successful, but the best.

This pressure has contributed to the escalation in the incidence of drug taking and the number of drug-related deaths within the sporting community.

© Australian Sports Drugs Agency (ASDA)

Olympic Charter against Doping in Sport

Preamble and principles

A. Considering that the use of doping agents is both unhealthy and contrary to the ethics of sport, and that it is necessary to protect the physical and spiritual health of athletes, the values of fair play and competition, the integrity and unity of sport, and the rights of those who participate in it at whatever level;

B. Considering that doping, as defined and adopted by the International Olympic Committee (IOC), is the administration or use of prohibited classes of drugs and of banned methods;

C. Considering that doping in sport is part of the problem of drug abuse and misuse in society;

D. Stating an unequivocal opposition to the use of, or encouragement or provision for the purpose of using doping agents and methods in sport;

E. Supporting the declaration made of athletes and coaches at Baden Baden in 1981 and of the IOC Athletes' Commission in Lausanne in 1985 calling for stronger doping controls and more severe sanctions;

F. Encouraged by the numerous initiatives taken by the sports movement and by governments to reduce doping in sport, and recognising that there has been considerable scientific progress in the detection and analysis of doping agents and methods;

G. Determined to prevent the spread of doping in sport to those countries and regions hitherto unaffected by the problem;

H. Esteeming that a commonly accepted international policy is necessary for elimination of doping in sport;

I. Considering that such a policy would lead to an improved and more consistent approach for the benefit of all sportsmen and sport-women, and would contribute to equality and equity in the international sporting community;

J. Considering that both public authorities and the independent sports organisations have separate but complementary responsibilities for the goal to eliminate doping in sport, and that a pre-requisite for success is that they should work together in co-operation and mutual respect for this purpose at all appropriate levels;

K. Recognising that the division of responsibilities in the implementation of this common policy will vary from country to country in accordance with its traditions, structures and laws, but sharing a common determination to ensure that it is carried through effectively and in accordance with acceptable standards of natural justice;

L. Stressing the need for consistent application by all the partners involved of the common anti-doping policy and strategy, particularly in elite sport;

M. Inviting the autonomous international sports federations to co-operate wholeheartedly in this policy and towards this end;

N. Inviting the IOC to take the leading role in securing approval of the Charter as well as in overseeing its implementation.

The countries and organisations which endorse this Charter hereby agree:

i) that the following elements are fundamental elements of a common anti-doping policy and strategy, and that they should be applied by governments and sports organisations, acting both individually and in co-operation,

ii) to implement those measures which are within their competence, and to encourage their partners to implement those which fall within their powers.

© *International Olympic Committee (IOC)*

Why do athletes use drugs?

Information from ASDA

There are a number of factors that may contribute to an athlete misusing drugs. These factors can be related to the drug itself, the person or their environment.

Drug
- effects of the drug
- ease of availability
- legal status
- physical dependence

Person
- dissatisfaction with performance and progress
- psychological dependence
- desire to cope with anxiety or stress
- desire to relax/socialise
- values – using drugs may not be considered a problem
- belief that others are using drugs
- temptation to think they can get away with it
- problem of being easily influenced by others
- lack of knowledge about side effects
- lack of confidence

Environment
- friends or other athletes using drugs
- culture of the sport
- pressure to win from coach, parents, public, media
- financial reward
- prestige and fame

- advertising
- influence of role models
- unrealistic qualifying standards or performance expectations
- national pride

Specific pressures

Self

The basic desire to be successful and satisfy ego requirements is a major source of internal pressure. Problems such as self-doubt, lack of confidence, nervousness, stress and depression are common to all athletes. The characteristics of self-pressure are not exclusive to people in the sporting field.

Coach

A successful athlete is often associated with a successful coach. As a result, the coach may place direct pressure on an athlete to perform and may be the source of further internal pressure.

Peer

Competitors set the standards to which an athlete must perform. If an athlete believes that a competitor has obtained some kind of advantage, then the pressure to also have or use this advantage is significant, for example, a better-designed golf club, a lighter running shoe or the use of

FOR AN ATHLETE – THE DIFFERENCE BETWEEN **SUCCESS** AND **FAILURE** CAN BE A MILLI-SECOND..

OR... AHEM, A MILLI-GRAM...

SK

steroids. Similar peer-group pressure may come from team mates.

Family
The expectations of family and friends are often a source of pressure, particularly at the lower levels of competition. Previously successful family members may also create pressure.

Spectators/crowd
Spectators create a great source of pressure both at the elite and lower levels of competition. At the elite level, athletes are often adopted as role models and will often take the hopes and aspirations of thousands of fans into competition.

Spectators are also the source of money and applause, hence the athlete may feel pressure to perform to standards expected by the public. The fickle nature of public support also creates pressure. Generally, we all love a winner and often adopt a 'win at all costs' mentality.

At the lower level of competition the presence of spectators may increase the anxiety levels of athletes. This may affect an athlete's performance and in due course influence an athlete's behaviour.

Media
The media plays an important role in shaping the opinions and attitudes of the general public. How the media portrays an athlete, and how they report on an athlete's performance, can not only influence the public but the athlete as well.

Administrators/promoters
Unreasonable scheduling of competitions and the establishment of unrealistic performance standards are ways in which sports administrators may contribute to the pressures on athletes. Similarly, promoters of sports events usually demand a high standard of performance from athletes to enhance the credibility and the promotional qualities of events which they sponsor.

Social
Pressure for sporting success may also be the result of social incentives to achieve. The glory and recognition for sporting achievements is a strong

Gender distribution of testing programme 1998/99

	No. Male samples	%	No. Female samples	%
Competition	2,531	80.6%	610	19.4%
Out-of-competition	1,622	80.9%	384	19.1%
Total	4,153	80.7%	994	19.3%

These percentages should be considered in terms of the number of males and females that participate in the sports that are included in the testing programme. Sports such as association football, cricket, equestrian racing, powerlifting and weight lifting are predominantly male based and it is these sports that make up the majority of the testing programme. This may suggest why the testing rate for males is significantly higher than that for females. These statistics will be monitored and kept under review.

Source: UK Sport

motivator towards success. Sporting success may provide an athlete with greater access and mobility to other social groups, that is, successful athletes are usually given the opportunity to meet and mix with people outside their usual social group, such as politicians and media personalities.

Financial and material rewards
Financial and material rewards are major influences on athletes and sporting performance. Sport, which was once an activity to fill in leisure time, has now become a way to earn a living for some of our elite athletes. In recent times people have commented that money-making principles have begun to replace athletes' moral principles.

Enormous salaries, product endorsements and potential careers outside of the sporting field are some of the rewards available to the successful athlete. Rewards are also available to athletes at lower levels of competition and to those in amateur sport. Even at junior levels, inducements such as scholarships are a significant incentive, and can increase the pressure to achieve.

National/political/ideological
Successful athletes at the highest level are sometimes elevated to the position of hero and carry the pressures of national honour and pride with them. Countries also use their athletes as political weapons. In international competition, one country's sporting successes over another country are often viewed as

proof of ideological or national superiority. Such is the case in the Olympic games, where enormous emphasis is placed on the number of gold medals won by a country, with even greater pressure being placed on the host country.

Factors such as an athlete's desire to win, the desire to please their coach and family, the glory of victory and the social and economic reward of sporting success often send the athlete in search of a competitive edge. Sometimes this search leads to the use of drugs.

Performance enhancement
What is doping?
Doping is the use by athletes of banned substances or methods that may enhance performance.

What is inadvertent doping?
Inadvertent doping occurs when an athlete uses a medication to treat an illness, without realising that it contains a banned substance, and consequently returns a positive drug-test result. In this situation, even though the athlete may not be taking drugs to enhance performance, they may return a positive drug-test result because the medication contains a banned substance.

Some examples of medications that contain banned substances are Sudafed and Demazin. In many cases your illness can be treated with an alternative medication that does not contain a banned substance.

© Australian Sports Drugs Agency (ASDA)

What is banned?

Information from the Sports Council for Wales

Athletes, of course, suffer from illnesses and are prone to develop muscular and skeletal injuries. It is vital, therefore, that clear guidance is given to athletes, so that they are aware of what they can and cannot take.

The whole subject of what is and is not banned is still a problem for both the IOC Medical Committee, which specifies the banned classes, and sports administrators, many of whom have little experience of dealing with such complicated issues.

Most governing bodies accept the IOC recommendations. A key difficulty is updating information when so many new drugs come onto the market and existing ones are withdrawn. It is difficult, therefore, to keep athletes fully up to date with the latest information.

The IOC goes some way to solving this problem by issuing a list of banned classes of drugs, though not a list of the drugs themselves, which would contain literally thousands of entries. An example of a banned class of drug is the Androgenic anabolic steroids. The IOC then gives examples, i.e. testosterone. Even then, it is not possible to list every example, so a rider is included – 'and related compounds' – which covers all similar drugs.

The responsibility for checking whether a drug is banned or not rests squarely with the athlete. The information on banned classes and examples should be provided by the sports' governing bodies. It is, in any case, available from the Sports Councils. The athlete needs to be sure that a drug is allowed before taking it.

Doping classes
- Stimulants
- Narcotics
- Anabolic agents
- Diuretics
- Peptide hormones, mimetics and analogues

Doping methods
- Blood doping
- Administering artificial oxygen carriers or plasma expanders
- Pharmacological, chemical and physical manipulation

Classes of drugs subject to certain restrictions
- Alcohol
- Cannabinoids
- Local anaesthetics
- Glucocorticosteroids
- Beta-blockers

Doping classes

Stimulants

Stimulants include drugs which increase alertness, reduce fatigue and may increase competitiveness and hostility. Their use can also produce loss of judgement, which may lead to accidents to the athletes themselves or to others. Amphetamine and related compounds have the most notorious reputation. Some deaths of sportsmen have resulted even when normal doses have been used under conditions of maximum physical activity. There is no medical reason for the use of amphetamines in sport.

One group of stimulants is the symphomimetic amines, of which ephedrine is an example. In high doses, this type of compound produces mental stimulation and increased blood flow. Adverse effects include high blood pressure and headache, increased and irregular heartbeat, anxiety and tremor. In lower doses, they are often in cold and hay fever preparations, which can be bought in pharmacies and sometimes other retail outlets without a medical prescription.

Beta 2 agonists

The choice of medication to treat asthma and respiratory ailments has posed many problems. Some years ago, ephedrine and related substances were taken quite often. However, these substances are banned because they are classed as 'symphathomimetic amines' and therefore considered as stimulants. However, salbutamol, salmeterol and terbutaline are permitted by inhaler only, to treat asthma. Prior notification of the use of one of these substances must be given to the relevant governing body.

Narcotic analgesics

The drugs in this class act specifically to control moderate to severe pain. This does not imply that their clinical effect is limited to the relief of trivial ailments. Most of these drugs have major side-effects, including dose-related respiratory depression, and carry a high risk of physical and psychological dependence. Evidence exists that narcotic analgesics have been and are abused in sports.

Anabolic agents

The androgenic anabolic steroids (AAS) class includes testosterone and related substances. They have been misused by the sports world to increase muscle strength and bulk, and to promote aggression. The use of AAS is associated with adverse effects on the liver, skin, cardio-vascular and endocrine systems. They can promote the growth of tumours and induce psychiatric syndromes. In males, use of AAS can decrease the size of the testes and diminish sperm production. Females experience masculinisation, loss of breast tissue and diminished menstruation. The use of AAS by teenagers can stunt growth.

Diuretics

Diuretics have important properties for eliminating fluids from tissues but strict medical control is needed. Diuretics are sometimes misused by competitors for two main reasons, namely: to lose weight quickly in sports where weight categories are involved and to reduce the concentration of drugs in urine by producing more rapid excretion to cut the risk of detection. Rapid loss of weight in sport cannot be justified medically and serious side-effects may occur.

Methods

Blood doping

Blood doping is the giving of blood or related red blood products to an athlete other than for legitimate medical treatment.

This practice goes against the ethics of medicine and sport. There are also risks involved in the transfusion of blood and related blood products. These include the develop-

ment of allergic reactions (rash, fever, etc.) and acute haemolytic reaction, with kidney damage if incorrectly typed blood is used, as well as delayed transfusion reaction resulting in fever and jaundice, transmission of infectious diseases (viral hepatitis and HIV) and metabolic shock.

Pharmacological, chemical and physical manipulation

The IOC Medical Commission bans the use of substances and methods that alter, or attempt to alter, the integrity and validity of the sample. Examples of banned methods are catheterisation, urine substitution and/or tampering and inhibition of renal excretion.

Classes of drugs subject to certain restrictions

Alcohol

Alcohol is not banned but breath or blood alcohol levels may be measured at the request of an International Federation, particularly in motorised sports.

Marijuana

Marijuana is not banned but tests may be carried out at the request of an International Federation.

The responsibility for checking whether a drug is banned or not rests squarely with the athlete

---

Local anaesthetics

Injectable local anaesthetics are permitted only under certain conditions.

Corticosteroids

The naturally-occurring and synthetic corticosteroids are mainly used as anti-inflammatory drugs which also relieve pain. They produce euphoria and side-effects and therefore need medical control. Since 1975, the IOC Medical Commission has tried to restrict their use during competition by requiring a declaration from team doctors. But, lately, stronger measures designed not to interfere with the appropriate medical use of these compounds have been introduced.

Glucocorticosteroids are prohibited when administered orally, rectally or by intravenous or intramuscular injection.

Beta-blockers

The IOC Medical Commission has reviewed the therapeutic uses of beta-blocking drugs and has found that there is now a wide range of effective alternatives to control hypertension, cardiac arrhythmias, angina pectoris and migraine. Due to the continued misuse of beta-blockers in some sports where physical activity is of little or no importance, the IOC Medical Commission reserves the right to carry out tests as it sees fit. These are unlikely to cover endurance events which demand prolonged periods of high cardiac output and in which beta-blockers would severely decrease performance.

And finally!

- Different sporting organisations may ban different drugs.
- Banned substances are found not only in medicines prescribed by doctors. They may be found in over-the-counter preparations.
- Medications from overseas should not be used unless they have been cleared with the governing body medical officer.
- Some so-called 'vitamin' preparations and nutritional supplements may contain banned substances.

© *Sports Council for Wales/UK Sport*

Prohibited classes of substances

Information from the IOC Medical Commission

Prohibited substances fall into the following classes of substances:

A. Stimulants
B. Narcotics
C. Anabolic agents
D. Diuretics
E. Peptide hormones, mimetics and analogues

A. Stimulants

Stimulants comprise various types of drugs which increase alertness, reduce fatigue and may increase competitiveness and hostility. Their use can also produce loss of judgement, which may lead to accidents to others in some sports. Amphetamine and related compounds have the most notorious reputation in producing problems in sport. Some deaths of sportsmen have resulted even when normal doses have been used under conditions of maximum physical activity. There is no medical justification for the use of amphetamines.

One group of stimulants is the sympathomimetic amines of which ephedrine, pseudoephedrine, phenyl-propanolamine and norpseudo-ephedrine are examples. In high doses, this type of compound produces mental stimulation and increased blood flow. Adverse effects include elevated blood pressure and headache, increased and irregular heart beat, anxiety and tremor. These compounds are often present in cold and hay fever preparations which can be purchased in pharmacies and sometimes from other retail outlets without a medical prescription.

Another group of stimulants is the beta-2 agonists. These drugs are unusual because they are classified as both stimulants and anabolic agents. When taken by mouth or by injection they exert powerful stimulatory and anabolic effects.

Oral and injectable administration of beta-2 agonists is banned.

Of the beta-2 agonists only Salbutamol and Terbutaline are permitted and only by inhalation.

Any physician wishing to administer beta-2 agonists by inhalation must give written notification prior to the competition to the relevant medical authority. The choice of medications to treat asthma and other common respiratory disorders poses problems because some of the more commonly prescribed drugs are powerful stimulants. Furthermore, because these drugs have many different product names, the status of a drug may be confusing. The most prudent approach is to never take or prescribe a product for colds, sore throats, and flu without first checking with a physician or pharmacist who has special expertise in this area.

B. Narcotics analgesics

Morphine and other compounds of this class are powerful analgesics and are mainly used for the management of severe pain. These drugs have major side-effects, including respiratory depression, and they carry a high risk of physical and psychological dependence. Evidence reveals that narcotic analgesics have been abused in sports. Therefore the IOC Medical Commission has issued and maintained a ban on their use. The ban is consistant with international restrictions and with the regulations and recommendations of the World Health Organisation regarding narcotics.

C. Anabolic agents

The anabolic class includes anabolic androgenic steroids (AAS) and beta-2 agonists.

Anabolic androgenic steroids (AAS).

The AAS class includes testosterone and substances that are related in structure and activity to it. They have been misused in sport to increase muscle strength and bulk, and to promote aggressiveness. The use of AAS is associated with adverse

effects on the liver, skin, cardio-vascular and endocrine systems. They can promote the growth of tumours and induce psychiatric syndromes. In males AAS decrease the size of the testes and diminish sperm production. Females experience masculinisation, loss of breast tissue and diminished menstruation. The use of AAS by teenagers can stunt growth.

D. Diuretics

Diuretics have important therapeutic indications for the elimination of excess body fluids from the tissues in certain pathological conditions and for management of high blood pressure.

Diuretics are sometimes misused by competitors for two main reasons, namely:
- to reduce weight quickly in sports where weight categories are involved and
- to reduce the concentration of drugs by diluting the urine.

Rapid reduction of weight in sport cannot be justified medically. Health risks are involved in such misuse because of serious side-effects which might occur.

Furthermore, deliberate attempts to reduce weight artificially in order to compete in lower weight classes or to dilute urine constitute clear manipulations which are unacceptable on ethical grounds.

For sports involving weight classes, the responsible authorities reserve the right to obtain urine samples from the competitor at the time of the weigh-in.

E. Peptide hormones, mimetics and analogues

1. Chorionic Gonadotrophin (HCG – human chorionic gonadotrophin): it is well known that the administration to males of Human Chorionic Gonadotrophin (HCG) and other compounds with related activity leads to an increased rate of production of endogenous androgenic steroids and is considered equivalent to the exogenous administration of testosterone.
2. Corticotrophin (ACTH): Corticotrophin has been misused to increase the blood levels of endogenous corticosteroids notably to obtain the euphoric effect of corticosteroids. The application of Corticotrophin is considered to be equivalent to the oral, intra-muscular or intravenous application of corticosteroids.
3. Growth hormone (HGH, somatotrophin): the misuse of Growth Hormone in sport is unethical and dangerous, because of various adverse effects, for example, cardiomiopathy, hypertension, diabetes mellitus, and acromegaly when given in high doses for a long period of time. Contamination of some growth hormone preparations of human origin can cause Creutzfeldt Jacob disease (a fatal neurological condition).

All the respective releasing factors of the above-mentioned substances are also banned.
4. Erythropoietin (EPO): this naturally occurring hormone is produced in the kidney and regulates red blood cell production. Synthetic EPO is currently available and has been demonstrated to induce changes similar to blood doping.

Prohibited methods

The following procedures are prohibited:

Blood doping

Blood transfusion is the intravenous administration of red blood cells or related blood products that contain red blood cells. Such products can be obtained from blood drawn from the same (autologous) or from a different (homologous) individual. The most common indications for red blood cell transfusion in conventional medical practice are acute blood loss and severe anaemia.

Blood doping is the administration of blood, red blood cells and related products to an athlete. This procedure may be preceded by withdrawal of blood from the athlete who continues to train in this blood-depleted state.

These procedures contravene the ethics of medicine and of sport. There are also risks involved in the transfusion of blood and related blood products. These include the development of allergic reactions (rash, fever etc.) and acute haemolytic reaction with kidney damage if incorrectly typed blood is used, as well as delayed transfusion reaction resulting in fever and jaundice, transmission of infectious diseases (viral hepatitis and AIDS), overload of the circulation and metabolic shock.

Therefore the practice of blood doping in sport is banned by the IOC Medical Commission.

Pharmaceutical, chemical and physical manipulation

Pharmacological, chemical and physical manipulation is the use of substances and of methods which alter, attempt to alter, or may reasonably be expected to alter the integrity and validity of samples used in doping controls. These include, without limitation, the administration of diuretics, catheterisation, sample substitution and/or tampering, inhibition of renal excretion such as by probenecid and related compounds, and alterations of testosterone and epitestosterone measurements such as epitestosterone* or bromantan administration.
* An epitestosterone concentration in the urine greater than 200 nanograms per millilitre will be investigated.

The IOC Medical Commission bans the use of substances and of methods which alter the integrity and validity of urine samples used in doping controls. Examples of banned methods are catheterisation, urine substitution and-or tampering, inhibition of renal excretion. e.g. by probenecid and related compounds, and epitestosterone administration. If the epitestosterone concentration is greater than 200 ng/ml, the laboratories should notify the appropriate authorities. The IOC Medical Commission recommends that under these circumstances further investigations be conducted.

The success or failure of the use of a prohibited substance or method is not material. It is sufficient that the said substance or procedure was used or attempted for the infraction to be considered as consummated.

© IOC Medical Commission
January, 2000

Classes of substances subject to certain restrictions

Alcohol

Alcohol is prohibited in some sports such as motor racing, shooting and fencing. Alcohol, in anything other than small quantities, depresses brain function which reduces tension, inhibition and self-control. As alcohol consumption continues, judgement, co-ordination and reactions are increasingly impaired.

Competitors could misuse alcohol for psychological reasons such as to increase confidence or reduce pain. It is more commonly used to reduce stress/tension and hand tremor which would be beneficial in sports requiring accuracy such as shooting and archery.

Alcohol can also have a deleterious effect on sporting performance as it can impair judgement, co-ordination and reaction time. It can also increase self-confidence resulting in an increased chance of taking a risk or acting in a way that the competitor would not normally. This could put both the competitor and other competitors at risk.

The issue of alcohol misuse in sport is complex due to the widespread use (and abuse) of alcohol in the general community. Alcoholic beverages are often part of the culture, religion and social interaction in a community. Some sports that test for alcohol also include provision for providing counselling and other education initiatives for the competitor.

Tests may be carried out for the presence of ethanol. Check your governing body's anti-doping regulations to determine whether alcohol is prohibited in your sport.

Cannabis

Cannabis (marijuana and hashish) is prohibited in some sports such as association football, swimming, motor cycling and rugby league. Cannabis is generally not considered performance enhancing, and could even be detrimental to performance. The use of cannabis may not be intended to improve performance. However, irrespective of the intention behind the use, if it is prohibited by a governing body's regulations an offence has been committed and therefore will be subject to disciplinary action.

The use of cannabis may be damaging to the image of sport and as elite competitors can be influential role models for young people the use of an illegal substance also sends inappropriate messages to them. For this reason some sports have prohibited the use of social drugs such as cannabis. The action taken by governing bodies who specifically test for social drugs may include rehabilitation and/or counselling to assist competitors to overcome their drug problems.

Cannabis is a hallucinogen. In small amounts it causes a feeling of relaxation, reduces inhibitions and results in a loss of perception of time and space. It also can result in impaired co-ordination and reduced ability to perform complex skills. Large amounts can impair mental functioning. These effects could obviously be detrimental to a competitor's ability to perform complex skills as well as place other competitors at risk. Cannabis could be used to reduce apprehension and to steady the nerves. Cannabis is illegal in the UK, therefore the production, supply, possession and use of this substance is against the law.

Alcohol can also have a deleterious effect on sporting performance as it can impair judgement, co-ordination and reaction time

---

Tests may be carried out for the presence of cannabinoids. Check your governing body's anti-doping regulations to determine whether cannabis is prohibited in your sport. At the Olympic Games, tests will be conducted for cannabinoids – a concentration in the urine greater than 15 nanograms per millilitre is prohibited.

Local anaesthetics

What are local anaesthetics?

Local anaesthetics are substances that produce the temporary loss of feeling. They are used medically for the control of pain.

Why might competitors use local anaesthetics to improve performance?

Competitors might use local anaesthetics to reduce or eliminate the pain felt from injury or illness so they can continue to compete or train.

What harm can local anaesthetics cause?

The use of local anaesthetics can result in the competitor continuing to train or compete when injured. The competitor may not realise the extent or severity of the injury and make the injury worse or cause permanent damage.

What types of medications contain local anaesthetics?

Local anaesthetics can be found in both prescription and over-the-counter medications. They may be found in creams, sprays, ear drops and eye drops as well as some sore throat products. These are permitted in sport.

Local anaesthetics are also administered by injection. Injectable local anaesthetics are only permitted under the following conditions:

a) that bupivacaine, lidocaine, mepivacaine, procaine etc. are used but not cocaine.

Vasoconstrictor agents (e.g. adrenaline) may be used in conjunction with local anaesthetics

b) only local or intra-articular injections may be administered

c) only when medically justified

Where the rules of a responsible authority so provide, notification of administration may be necessary.

Glucocorticosteroids

What are corticosteroids?

Corticosteroids are drugs derived from the corticosteroid hormone that is produced by the adrenal gland. Synthetic corticosteroids are also available.

What do corticosteroids do?

Corticosteroids are primarily used for their anti-inflammatory properties. However, when administered systemically they can produce a feeling of euphoria (increased feeling of well-being).

Corticosteroids are commonly used to treat asthma, hay fever, tissue inflammation, rheumatoid arthritis and inflammatory bowel disease.

What harm can corticosteroids cause?

Prolonged use of large doses of corticosteroids can cause:

- mood changes
- acne
- osteoporosis
- increased blood pressure
- peptic ulcers
- reduced effect of insulin

What types of medications contain corticosteroids?

Corticosteroids are available by prescription only and can be found in creams, ointments, inhalers as well as by injection or tablet. They are commonly found in asthma medications, hay fever preparations and creams/ointments for inflammatory skin disorders. Corticosteroids are also used by injection to treat inflammation of tissues.

The use of corticosteroids is prohibited when administered orally, rectally or by intravenous or intramuscular injection.

Therefore the following rates of administration are permitted:

- topical use (on the anus, ears, skin, nose and eyes) but not rectal. For example creams, ointments and eye drops
- by inhalation, e.g. Becotide, Pulmicort, Becloforte
- by intra-articular or local injection (injection into joint or soft tissue), e.g. cortisone, prednisolone.

Corticosteroids are prohibited in tablet or syrup form. Usually if a competitor reaches a stage that requires this form of administration, they are unlikely to be participating in high-level sport.

Beta Blockers

What are beta blockers?

Beta blockers block the transmission of stimuli through the beta receptors. They stop the actions of noradrenaline (increased heart rate, dilation of blood vessels – getting the body ready to act). Beta blockers are used medically to treat angina, high blood pressure, and heart disease. They may also be used in the treatment of migraines and to reduce the symptoms of anxiety.

What do beta blockers do?

Beta blockers reduce the heart rate and the force at which the heart contracts as well as preventing dilation of the blood vessels. Preventing dilation of the blood vessels contributes to reducing the work load of the heart.

Why might competitors use beta blockers to improve performance?

Competitors may misuse beta blockers to decrease heart rate, steady nerves and stop trembling. Decreasing heart rate would increase the amount of time between each beat of the heart which in turn could allow a competitor to perform their skill without the heart beat compromising accuracy. This would be an advantage in sports requiring a great degree of accuracy such as shooting and archery.

Beta blockers could also be used to reduce anxiety of a competitor.

What types of medications contain beta blockers?

Beta blockers can be found in medications used to treat angina, high blood pressure, heart disease and migraine and are only available on prescription.

Some examples of medications containing beta blockers include:

- Tenormin (atenolol)
- Beta-Prograne (propranolol)
- Inderal LA (propranolol)

• The above information is from UK Sport, see page 41 for address details.

Narcotic analgesics

Information from UK Sport

What are narcotic analgesics?

Narcotic analgesics are painkillers. They are used in medicine to relieve pain. Narcotic analgesics are the strongest form of painkillers.

What do narcotic analgesics do?

Narcotic analgesics act on the brain and spinal cord to reduce the amount of pain felt.

Why might competitors use narcotic analgesics to improve performance?

Competitors might use narcotic analgesics to reduce or eliminate the pain felt from injury or illness or to increase the pain threshold so they can continue to compete or train. This can result in the competitor continuing the activity and not realising the extent or severity of the injury. This can make the injury worse or cause permanent damage.

There are also international restrictions regarding supply and possession of narcotics. In the UK many of the drugs in this class are controlled by the Misuse of Drugs Act 1971 which controls the import/export, manufacturing, supply and possession of these substances.

What harm can narcotic analgesics cause?

Narcotic analgesics may produce a feeling of euphoria as well as reduce mental capacity. This could result in a false feeling of invincibility and that the competitor's ability is better than it actually is, or the perception of dangerous situations as safe and therefore put themselves and other competitors at risk.

The misuse of narcotic analgesics may cause:

- drowsiness
- decreased breathing rate
- nausea and vomiting
- constipation
- sweating
- loss of concentration, balance and co-ordination

Fainting, palpitations, sedation, restlessness and mood changes are also side-effects of narcotic analgesics. Narcotic analgesics are highly addictive.

Overdose of narcotic analgesics can result in coma and breathing difficulties that often results in death. Long-term abuse often results in reduced mental and physical capacity.

Some of the substances prohibited under this category may be administered intravenously which can increase the risk of serious health problems including transmission of infectious diseases such as hepatitis and HIV.

What types of medications contain narcotic analgesics?

Narcotic analgesics can be found in both prescription and over-the-counter medications. Medications used for moderate to severe pain relief, such as morphine, diamorphine (heroin) and pethidine are available on prescription only.

Preparations for mild pain relief as well as cough/cold and stomach disorders such as diarrhoea may contain mild analgesics such as codeine. They are often found in combination with aspirin (permitted), paracetamol (permitted) or caffeine (restricted). These can be purchased over-the-counter without prescription.

Some examples of medications containing prohibited narcotic analgesics include:

- Diocalm (morphine sulphate)
- Palfium (dextromoramide)
- Pethidine
- Sevredol (morphine sulphate)

Examples of narcotic analgesics include:

- buprenorphine
- dextromoramide
- diamorphine (heroin)
- hydrocodone
- morphine
- methadone
- pentrazocine
- pethidine

…and related substances

Please note that aspirin, codeine, dextromethorphan, dextropropoxyphene, dihydrocodeine, diphenoxylate, ethylmorphine, pholcodine, propoxyphene, paracetamol and tramadol are permitted.

Non-steroidal anti-inflammatory drugs

Non-steroidal anti-inflammatory drugs (NSAIDs) are also used to manage pain (usually mild to moderate pain) as well as to reduce swelling and stiffness. These drugs have pain relieving and anti-inflammatory properties. NSAIDs are commonly used for the management of arthritis, back pain, soft tissue injuries and menstrual pain.

NSAIDs are permitted in sport.

Some examples of NSAIDs include:

- Brufen or Advil (ibuprofen)
- Feldene (piroxicam)
- Naprosyn (naproxen)
- Ponstan Forte (mefenamic acid)

© UK Sport

Anabolic androgenic steroids

Information from UK Sport

Drugs are intended to treat people with medical ailments. Used properly, drugs can save lives. Nevertheless, any drug can be dangerous especially when taken for a long time and in high doses. Doctors take these risks into consideration when prescribing treatments.

The use of substances or methods to enhance performance is cheating, unfair and is contrary to the spirit of fair competition. Drug misuse can be harmful to the athlete's health or to other athletes competing in the sport. It severely damages the integrity, image and value of sport, whether or not the motivation to use drugs is to improve performance.

Substances and methods are prohibited in sport for various reasons including performance-enhancing effects, health of the athlete and legality. One class of substances prohibited in sport is the anabolic agents. The anabolic agents class includes anabolic androgenic steroids.

What are anabolic androgenic steroids?

Anabolic androgenic steroids are natural or man-made compounds that act in a similar way to the hormone testosterone. Testosterone is a male sex hormone that is produced by the testes. It is also found in women in small quantities and is produced by the ovaries and the adrenal gland.

Anabolic steroids have been used medically for the treatment of some forms of anaemia (to stimulate blood cell production), osteoporosis and to promote recovery after a serious illness or major surgery. They have also been used in the treatment of breast cancer and for boys/men who are deficient in the naturally occurring male sex hormones.

In the UK, anabolic steroids are classified as a Class C drug under the Misuse of Drugs Act 1971. It is an offence to produce, supply, possess or import/export anabolic steroids with intent to supply. However, it is not an offence to possess them when in a form of a medicinal product for personal use.

There are many different anabolic steroids available throughout the world. Some examples include Nandrolene, Stanozolol, Testosterone, Boldenone, Androstenedione, Androstenediol and DHEA. Some of the anabolic steroids used have been designed for veterinary use. Anabolic steroids are available in tablet form or for intramuscular injection, under trade names such as Dianabol, Durabolin, Deca-Durabolin, Winstrol and Anavar. Some substances prohibited under the anabolic agents class may be found in nutritional products such as androstenedione and DHEA.

What do anabolic androgenic steroids do?

Testosterone is responsible for stimulating the development of male sexual characteristics (the androgenic effect) and the build-up of muscle tissue (anabolic effect). Anabolic androgenic steroids are natural or man-made compounds that act in a similar way to testosterone.

Most manufacturers of anabolic steroids attempt to minimise the androgenic and maximise the anabolic effects of the drug. All available anabolic steroids have both actions to a varying degree according to the body's own response. Anabolic androgenic steroids are often referred to as 'anabolic steroids' – both names refer to the same substances.

Why might competitors use anabolic androgenic steroids to improve performance?

Competitors use anabolic androgenic steroids to improve sporting performance, and in particular to:
- increase muscle size, strength and power
- to train harder and for longer
- to increase aggression and competitiveness

The androgenic effects of anabolic steroids (increased aggression and competitiveness) help the competitor to train harder and to recover more quickly, resulting in increased strength.

There is little evidence to support the belief that anabolic steroids alone can increase muscle strength in adult males – development is dependent on an appropriate diet and exercise programme. When anabolic steroids are used without training, muscles tend to look bigger, but this is probably due to water retention. Because of their ability to promote the quality and quantity of training, anabolic steroids became known as 'training drugs', taken during training before a competition. To reduce the risk of being caught by a drug test, the competitor comes off the drugs several weeks before a competition and may retain some of the benefits. However, anabolic steroids have always been detected during competition testing as well as during out-of-competition testing, showing the extent of the risk that some competitors are prepared to take.

What harm can anabolic steroids cause?

Anabolic steroids mimic hormones that are naturally occurring in the body, and therefore can interfere with the normal hormone balance in the body as well as their actions. This

> *The use of substances or methods to enhance performance is cheating, unfair and is contrary to the spirit of fair competition*

13

interference can cause adverse side-effects ranging from development of male features in females, loss of fertility and eventual impotence in males to acne and kidney damage. They can also increase blood pressure, cause hardening of the arteries and increase the risk of heart disease. Anabolic steroids also increase the risk of liver disease and certain forms of cancer.

Potential harmful side-effects of anabolic steroid misuse include:

In males
- acne
- increased aggression and sexual appetite
- long-term use can result in sterility and impotence
- reduced sperm production

- shrinking and hardening of the testicles
- kidney damage
- development of breasts*
- premature baldness
- prostate enlargement

In females
- acne
- development of male features including facial hair
- deepening of the voice*
- irregular periods
- more hair growth on the face and body*
- increased aggression and sexual appetite
- enlargement of the clitoris*

In adolescents
- severe acne on the face and body
- a male-like physique in girls

- stunted growth due to premature closure of the growth centres of the bones*

* side-effects may be permanent

Anabolic steroids can also reduce the body's ability to cope with physical stress and over-exertion which may result in overheating or excessive fatigue.

Some anabolic steroids are injected which will also increase the risk of serious problems including transmission of infectious diseases such as hepatitis and HIV. Other problems associated with the use of anabolic steroids is their supply on the black market which has dangers in that they may be fakes or contain impurities or additives which can cause serious and even fatal side-effects.

© UK Sport

Why should sport be drug free?

The use of doping substances or doping methods to enhance performance is cheating, unfair and contrary to the sprit of fair competition. Drug misuse can be harmful to the competitors health or to other competitor's competing in the sport. It severely damages the integrity, image and value of sport, whether or not the motivation to use drugs is to improve performance.

Substances and methods are prohibited in sport for various reasons including:
- performance-enhancing effects – which contravene the ethics of sport and undermine the principles of fair participation.
- health of the competitor – some drug misuse may cause serious side-effects which can compromise a competitor's health. Using substances to mask pain/injury could make an injury worse or cause permanent damage. Some drug misuse can be harmful to other competitors participating in the sport.
- legality – some substances are forbidden by law to possess or supply them.

Most sporting federations have anti-doping regulations to ensure all competitors compete under the same rules. The regulations aim to achieve drug-free sport through clearly stated policies, testing, sanctions and preventative education. They are also intended to raise the awareness of drug misuse and deter competitors from misusing prohibited drugs and methods.

Competitors can be influential role models for young people. The behaviour of elite competitors can have a significant impact on young people as they admire and aspire to emulate their sporting heroes, especially their actions and attitudes. High-profile competitors should remember that they are regularly in the media and their actions can and do impact on many people.

The use of illegal drugs brings all sport into disrepute and can ruin a sporting career

---

The use of illegal drugs brings all sport into disrepute and can ruin a sporting career. For this reason some sports have banned the use of 'social drugs' such as marijuana. Other 'social drugs' such as cocaine, amphetamines or heroin are banned by all sports. The action taken by governing bodies who test specifically for 'social drugs' can include rehabilitation and treatment to assist competitors to overcome their drug problems.

Sport is about competing and performing to the best of your ability. If you, your coach or medical adviser resort to using drugs to assist your performance, you are also cheating yourself. And if you are caught breaking the rules, you could affect your sporting career as well as bring shame on your sport, family and friends.

Be one of the competitors who performs well in sport without using drugs. Be proud to be drug free.
- The above is an extract from *Competitors' and Officials' Guide to Drugs and Sport*, produced by UK Sport.

© UK Sport

Drugs in sport

The issues explained

By Harriet Sherwood

Why is athlete Mark Richardson in trouble?

He has tested positive for a banned substance called nandrolone. Richardson denies having done anything illegal, but admits that he ignored advice to stop taking nutritional supplements, which may contain nandrolone. In the two hours before giving his positive urine samples, he took a cocktail of supplements including acetyl-glutamine (to boost the immune system), Promax-159 (a protein-rich liquid), and Viper (an isotonic energy drink which replaces lost fluids). Richardson says in future he would not take supplements.

What is nandrolone?

It's an anabolic steroid which pumps up muscle bulk. Bodybuilders use it to achieve dramatic muscle definition, while power lifters use it to get their biceps to a maximum bulk. All anabolic steroids have a role to play in producing testosterone, the natural hormone that produces spurts of growth at puberty. Testosterone is also linked with aggression, another useful quality for competitors.

How does nandrolone work?

Anabolic steroids increase the proportion of protein laid down as muscle tissue and stimulate bone growth. They also stimulate the production of red blood corpuscles which in turn enhance the oxygen supply to the muscles.

Do they have any other effects?

They can be dangerous, especially to children and adolescents, and even for healthy adults they have some undesirable side-effects – lowered fertility but raised sex drive, shrinking testicles, raised blood pressure, headaches, nausea and a range of psychological symptoms including impulsive aggression and emotional instability.

Do anabolic steroids have legitimate uses?

They can help patients on dialysis, slow weight loss in HIV-positive women, relieve distress in jaundice and help in cases of life-threatening anaemia.

What are the rules for athletes?

Obviously, any athlete using anabolic steroids is likely to have an advantage over an athlete who doesn't. The International Amateur Athletics Federation (IAAF) sets international rules, and has banned all use of anabolic steroids. Athletic bodies in individual countries are required to implement rules and test athletes for illicit substances. In this country, UK Sport carries out random testing of all athletes. The high number of positive tests over recent years has led a number of athletes' organisations to call for further investigation into anabolic steroids.

Why the controversy?

A number of sportsmen and women have tested positive in the past few years, many of whom have denied any wrongdoing. Some have claimed that nandrolone could be present in fruit and vegetables or red meat. But a committee set up by UK Sport to investigate nandrolone concluded that many of the health supplements which have recently flooded the market could be to blame. 'Some dietary supplements contain compounds similar to nandrolone or its metabolic precursors, which produce the same metabolites as does nandrolone,' said Professor Vivian James of the University of London, who led the inquiry. Some athletes could have taken supplements without knowing the risks or may have been misled by manufacturers.

Who else apart from Mark Richardson has tested positive?

Most famously, the athlete Linford Christie, who was cleared of any wrongdoing. Athletes Dougie Walker and Gary Cadogan also tested positive but were later cleared. French footballer Christophe Dugarry, Spencer Smith, Britain's former world triathlon champion, and Merlene Ottey, the Jamaican sprinter, have also tested positive but say they are innocent. Boxer Jon Thaxton was recently banned for nine months after testing positive. The former Australian open champion Petr Korda was banned from playing professional tennis for two years. He was later cleared on appeal.

Is it possible that athletes' samples have been spiked?

Athletes often use that defence, but it has only ever once been proved successful. In 1995 hurdler Lydumila Enquist had a four-year suspension lifted after her husband admitted to a Russian court that he had spiked his wife's food with anabolic steroids in a fit of jealousy after she had asked him for a divorce.

Where do you get hold of anabolic steroids and dietary supplements?

Anabolic steroids are prescription-only medicines, and it is illegal to supply them, though not to possess them. Mark Richardson says the three nutritional supplements which he took were bought from Maximuscle of north London, a supplier of sports supplements. Most of them come from the US, and are often sold by health food suppliers as well as specialist sports retailers. Supplements – many openly containing nandrolone – are available on the net. GNC, the health-and-diet retail chain, stopped stocking the products some time ago, saying it was more than their reputation was worth.

© The Guardian February, 2000

Nowhere to run

Our expectations are putting athletes in an impossible position

Once again we are in the middle of scandal and controversy over the use of drugs in sport and the incredible pressure on athletes to succeed.

In Britain, Linford Christie, the 1992 100-metre Olympic champion and vociferous opponent of drug use, has tested positive for the steroid nandrolone. He protests his innocence and, judging by the press reaction, the public are ready to believe their icon. And they have a precedent. Scottish sprinter Dougie Walker earlier tested positive for the same drug but was cleared by British athletics' governing body last month.

Why can't sensitive tests using sophisticated mass spectrometers simply show whether an athlete is guilty or not? The sad answer is that there is an arms race going on between the drug-testing laboratories and manufacturers of substances designed to boost sporting performance. And it's an arms race that can never end because, as we know more about the biology of sports performances, it will grow easier to change athletes' bodies undetectably by boosting levels of naturally occurring hormones.

Right now, the situation for athletes is particularly difficult because of the sheer number of sports supplements, including natural products, which may or may not have an effect that a drug test would pick up. At the same time, the list of drugs that could get an athlete into trouble has grown enormous – the Canadian Center for Drug-Free Sports, for example, lists over 500 banned medicines. And the International Olympic Committee, which sets drug-testing standards, is not helping much. Instead of openly resolving controversy over what test results for steroids really mean, it is adding to the confusion by refusing proper scientific debate over its studies.

But nothing will change the real issue. The public expects athletes to break records and rewards them with fame and fortune when they do. At the same time, it is becoming more and more impossible for athletes to set those new records without that little extra help.

The graphs on this page make it clear just how difficult progress in track and field sports has become. Take the 100-metre sprint as the ultimate example. At the first modern Olympic Games held in Athens in 1896, the sprint was won by Thomas Burke of the US in a now-leisurely 12 seconds. Eight years later, Archie Hahn stripped a whole second from the record at St Louis.

The bottom line is that in striving for new records, modern athletes are no longer just competing against each another but against all the great athletes who ever lived

---

But it then took another twenty years to knock off a further 0.4 seconds. At Paris in 1924, the British runner Harold Abrahams reached 10.6 seconds in the race that was later celebrated in the movie *Chariots of Fire*. The next 0.4 seconds had to wait until the 1960 Rome Olympics.

Since then, progress has grown ever slower. Over the past three Olympics, the focus has shifted to slicing off hundredths of a second. Carl Lewis reached 9.92 at Seoul in 1988, Christie won with a slower time of 9.96 at Barcelona, and then Donovan Bailey hit a new record of 9.84 at Atlanta in 1996. The one outrider, of course, is Ben Johnson. He finished in a shattering 9.79 seconds at Seoul back in 1988 but was disqualified when he tested positive for steroids.

The story is much the same for all the track and field sports whether they need speed, endurance or strength. Graphs for the shot put show huge improvements initially (especially for women once they were allowed to compete in the Olympics) followed by a plateau.

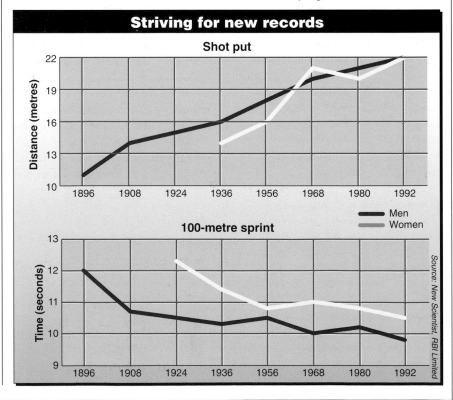

Striving for new records

Shot put

100-metre sprint

Men
Women

Source: New Scientist, RBI Limited

The bottom line is that in striving for new records, modern athletes are no longer just competing against each another but against all the great athletes who ever lived. The temptation to go faster with drugs is enormous.

And the opportunity is certainly there. Five minutes on the Internet will turn up sources for hundreds of nutritional supplements and 'natural' steroids, alongside banned drugs like nandrolone. Beyond these are the more sophisticated drugs like genetically-engineered erythropoetin, which increases red blood cell count, human growth hormone and then peptide hormones and the releasing factors for them.

Tiny quantities of drug have the potential to manipulate natural body processes and detection becomes still harder.

This arms race will undoubtedly escalate. As long as we expect sporting heroes to perform miracles, how could it be otherwise?

© New Scientist, RBI Limited
14 August 1999

Thin legal line in going for gold

Even wary athletes fall foul of the banned substances' list with dangers lurking in health preparations and meat

In the highly pressurised world of athletics, where a fraction of a second can mean the difference between ignominy and glory, athletes are continually finding themselves at the centre of a battle to run that little bit faster, jump that little bit higher and train that little bit harder.

The financial rewards for those who succeed can be considerable and the methods used by many to acquire that success are becoming increasingly elaborate as they go in search of the ultimate peformance.

For most athletes, sport is not just about training five times a week but also about nutrition. Many have to tread a thin line over what their bodies can and cannot consume if they are to pass the regular drug tests that have become part of modern sport.

In Britain, athletes are tested by officals from the UK Sports Council, which produces a detailed guide on what is banned.

While the number of random, out-of-competition tests has increased over the past few years, the problem facing athletes and testers alike is the growth of a grey area surrounding banned substances.

Excessive amounts of tea and coffee can lead to an athlete failing a drugs test, as can some painkillers, while the case of European 200-metre champion Dougie Walker, which involved – like the Linford Christie case – nandrolone, showed how many banned substances could exist in modern foods.

By Vivek Chaudhary, Sports Correspondent

One of the theories put forward during Walker's case was that European cattle were regularly fed with nandrolone and other anabolic steroids and this was passed on to the athlete when he ate the meat. It was a defence that was successfuly used in 1997 by the British bobsleigh racer Lenny Paul, who also claimed after failing a drugs test that he had eaten meat contaminated with steroids.

Legal dilemmas

The UK Sports Council lists a number of prohibited substances for athletes including stimulants; narcotic analgesics, which are found in the strongest types of painkillers; anabolic agents such as different types of steroids; diuretics which are used by doctors to treat high blood pressure and kidney and heart diseases; and various types of hormones. But the

For most athletes, sport is not just about training five times a week but also about nutrition. Many have to tread a thin line over what their bodies can and cannot consume

five banned classes of substances contain within them hundreds of other substances that athletes should not take.

Each of the substances can have a different impact on an athlete's physique and performance but, as sports administrators and athletes themselves point out, they can also be found in a number of other products.

For example, caffeine is a prohibited substance when used in large quantities. UK Sports Council guidelines state that the concentration of caffeine in the urine should not exceed 12 micrograms per millilitre and this also applies to tea, chocolate products and some soft drinks.

Other high-profile sports stars who have also recently tested positive for nandrolone include tennis player Petr Korda and French footballer Christophe Dugarry. They were both later cleared, leading to claims that like Walker they were using a health supplement that contained the banned steroid or could have eaten contaminated meat.

In the drive to improve performances, and cash in on the lucrative sponsorship deals that success brings, athletes in particular are constantly on the lookout for legal substances that will help them. Consequently the health supplement industry has become one of the fastest growing in the world of sport, worth an estimated £12.7 billion. The attraction of health supplements is that they are not prescribed and are seen as natural ways of enhancing performance.

Walker and Korda both claimed that they had taken a supplement called androstenedione, which helps develop muscles and aids training but also contains an off-shoot of nandrolone, something they claimed they were not aware of.

Another popular supplement – which is legal and has not been found to contain any banned substances – is creatine, which is used by the England football team, a number of leading Premier League clubs and athletes such as Linford Christie and Colin Jackson.

The products on offer to athletes are becoming increasingly sophisticated, making the job of the UK Sports Council's testers, who tour the country carrying out random tests throughout the year, more difficult. Steve Bird, a sports scientist at Canterbury Christ Church college and a former Sports Council tester, said the increase in the grey area of performance-enhancing substances has increased the difficulties for athletes.

He said: 'There have been a number of athletes who have tested positive for nandrolone, much more than previous years. It's either a case of them taking it with a little less discretion or accidentally taking it via a health supplement or even meat.

'The presence of steroids in meat has been of concern for quite some time but what's not quite clear is how much meat you would have to eat for the steroids to show up in an athlete's urine. The growth in this grey area makes it much harder for the tribunals that sit to judge an athlete's case when they have tested positive because they have to try to establish how it might have got there.'

The problem facing many athletes is that not all products, like vitamin and health supplements, clearly list their contents.

Mr Bird said: 'Athletes are not chemists and it's not always immediately obvious what's banned.'

Mr Bird believes that all supplements used by athletes should be labelled more clearly while more information needs to be made available to them on what they can and cannot take.

Once an athlete has tested positive, a tribunal is assembled to investigate the case and pass judgment. For sports governing bodies, however, with many athletes able to show that they were not aware that they were taking a banned substance, the outcome is usually a legal writ. Until the tribunal reaches its decision, athletes are banned, depriving them of income. Walker is estimated to have lost around £50,000 during the period he was temporarily banned from athletics.

The most famous doping case is that of Diane Modahl, who was sent home from the Commonwealth Games in 1994 when she failed a drugs test. She was cleared two years later and her subsequent legal action against the British Athletic Federation forced the organisation into administration because of the costs involved in fighting the case. The case is due to be heard at the high court later this year.

© The Guardian
August, 1999

Nandrolone, the sportsman's favourite performance drug

By Tim Radford, Science Editor

Nandrolone is an anabolic steroid manufactured and sold under the name Deca-Durabolin. It is, in various combinations, the body builder's favourite because it pumps up muscle bulk. 'It has proven to be an excellent product for promoting size and strength gains,' says one supplier's blurb, which adds coyly that the drug unfortunately has very stubborn metabolites which might show up in a steroid test even 12 months after injection. 'For those whose worries do not include steroid testing,' it continues, 'it remains the number one choice.'

Body builders use it to achieve dramatic muscle definition, while power lifters use it to get their biceps to a maximum bulk, although they could risk disqualification.

All anabolic steroids have a role to play in producing testosterone, the natural hormone that produces spurts of growth at puberty; testosterone is also linked with aggression, another useful quality for competitors.

Since such drugs mimic or enhance natural processes, the evidence from blood or urine tests may sometimes be ambiguous, and the decision can depend on levels of these tell-tale substances in the bloodstream, rather than simply their presence. Steroid-based medical treatments are sometimes used for limb or joint injuries, and chemical derivatives of anabolic steroids are sometimes found in dietary preparations for athletes and body builders: these might leave traces in the bloodstream or urine.

Anabolic steroids increase the proportion of protein laid down as muscle tissue and stimulate bone growth. They also stimulate the production of red blood corpuscles which in turn enhance the oxygen supply to the muscles.

Anabolic steroids are prescription-only medicines, and in Britain it is illegal to supply them, though not to possess them. They can be dangerous, especially to children and adolescents, and even for healthy adults they have some undesirable side-effects – lowered fertility but raised sex drive, shrinking testicles, raised blood pressure, headaches, nausea and a range of psychological symptoms including impulsive aggression and emotional instability.

But they have also helped patients on dialysis, they have slowed weight loss in HIV-positive women, they can relieve distress in jaundice and help in cases of life-threatening anaemia.

© The Guardian
August, 1999

What's it all about?

By Simon Hughes

Are you one of those people, like me, whose eyes glaze over when the subject of nandrolone abuse crops up? Well, you're in excellent company. Various highly-qualified professors of chemistry, biochemistry and pharmaceutics have spent months studying the issue, and they don't understand it either.

It is one of those subjects, like the war in Bosnia or the European single currency, that's got so intricate and involved, that we men/women in the street (never mind the beleaguered scientists) have become fairly detached from it.

It might be practical, therefore, to sift through all the flotsam, and get to the nub. So here goes . . .

Let's start with the basics. Nandrolone is an anabolic steroid, an organic compound closely related to the male hormone testosterone. It is made in a complex chemical process, sometimes using part of the Mexican agare plant. In medicine, it is injected into patients to treat breast cancer, some blood disorders, and to rebuild muscles after debilitating diseases. It is the latter property that has attracted athletes to it for the past 25 years. It promotes muscle growth and aids recovery after strenuous training sessions. Not only is it banned by the International Olympic Committee, it is also illegal out of the hands of qualified medical practitioners.

Various chemical laboratories, however, have been clever. They have developed other products, taken in pill form as a food supplement, that when swallowed react in the body to form nandrolone internally, offering the taker all its supposed muscular benefits. They are called things like Androdiol and Andro Gen and are legally sold in certain fitness shops. The pills contain two other steroids, kind of seeds of nandrolone, we'll call Nor 1 and Nor 2. These steroids are also now banned by the IOC.

International athletes are regularly drug-tested, both during training and at events. Tamper-proof, sophisticated analysis of their urine is conducted, in Britain, at a smart King's College lab in London. If the waste-product 19-norandrosterone is detected in the urine, this is proof that nandrolone has been in the athlete's body. If there is more than two nanograms of the waste-product per millilitre of urine, the male athlete has failed the test. (For women, the threshold is 5ng/ml.)

The problem for the testers is that they can't be sure how the nandrolone got there. A comprehensive, independent survey carried out in the last six months by a team of British scientists identified four possible sources:

1. It could have been injected (nandrolone can remain in the body for up to a year). This is extremely unlikely, as all top athletes would know the consequences.
2. It could have come from eating a large quantity of wild boar offal, which is known to contain nandrolone. Also unlikely.
3. The athlete might have taken pills or eaten food containing Nor 1 or Nor 2. He may have known of these steroids' presence, or he may not have.
4. Minute amounts of nandrolone are known to exist naturally in the human body (especially in pregnant women) but widespread testing has found the waste-product never exceeds 0.6ng/1000ml in men, and rarely exceeds 0.1ng.

So all roads lead to source 3. That is where the problems really start. The tarnished athletes plead innocence. Some may have a case. There are herbal food supplements and other pills made by unrecognised companies that don't declare all their ingredients. There are a few pirates out there, and other products can be ambiguous.

Yesterday, I checked out the shop Body Active in a dingy subway opposite Charing Cross station in

I'M AFRAID THAT YOUR URINE SAMPLE SHOWED—

—I TOLD THE COACH THAT ALL THAT HEALTH FOOD STUFF TASTED LIKE BOAR OFFAL!!

London. It displays a bewildering array of pills and powders for sale. Some, like 19-NOR from the British company Maximuscle, do declare in the small print that they contain steroids and should not be taken by IOC competitors. It sells 5,000 jars a month. Others, such as Androdiol made by the US company Genetic Evolutionary Nutrition, list the incomprehensible chemical ingredients, but do not carry any cautionary advice.

The sudden surge of nandrolone stories is not just media hyperbole. From 1990 to 1998, there was an average of four positive readings per year in Britain. In 1999 there were 17 instances of positive readings. Even allowing for a slightly larger sample, it is an alarming jump. I asked Professor Vivian James, an expert on steroids who chaired the survey on nandrolone, why there had been this sudden rash of cases.

'I just don't know,' he said. 'I'm as baffled as anyone. The testing procedure is certainly foolproof.'

There have certainly been some choice excuses from the athletes. Lenny Paul, the British bobsleigher, claimed his positive test was the result of eating spaghetti bolognese. Germany's Dieter Baumann claimed his toothpaste had been spiked. Others point the finger at the tablets they take, blaming their inaccurate labelling.

Clearly there is peer pressure among athletes to augment their diet with pills and potions; when one fails a nandrolone test, either he or his supplier is not telling the truth.

There is now a clamour from leading scientists for a proper investigation into food supplements. It will not be easy, bearing in mind that poachers tend to stay one step ahead of gamekeepers. For the moment an international athlete's body will remain a temple . . . of pharmaceutics.

• First appeared in *The Daily Telegraph*.
© *Simon Hughes*

Nandrolone crisis

In search of truth

By Sue Mott

British athletics is in the dock. The widespread perception that the sport has a drug problem has been fuelled by the latest flurry of nandrolone cases and *The Electronic Telegraph* has learned that there have been a number of other positive tests which may give rise to further investigation.

The man required to stand up against the waves of public suspicion now breaking over his sport is David Moorcroft, the chief executive of UK Athletics, who, he freely admits, failed his maths, law and chemistry O-levels. He has certainly enrolled on a crash course now.

Ever since British 400-metre runner Mark Richardson tested positive for metabolites of the anabolic steroid nandrolone, like Doug Walker, Gary Cadogan and Linford Christie – all of whom have protested their innocence – Moorcroft has been dealing in nanograms, legal niceties, innuendo and a climate of distrust.

He could be forgiven for mistaking his Birmingham office for a bunker, so great has been the flak flying in his direction. Instead, he has volunteered for extra head-above-the-parapet duties. His desire, he explains, is to let the truth – whether it be exoneration or condemnation – be told.

The credibility of athletics is at stake. Do you really believe there is an innocent explanation for everyone who tests positive for drugs in this country or can you countenance the possibility of guilt?
It's possible the tests do indicate guilt, yes. It is conceivable that some of them are guilty, that all of them are guilty or that – possibly – none of them are. It's also possible that research will show that poorly labelled food supplements do trigger a metabolic response in the body that creates nandrolone metabolites.

But one of the things we've got to consider, possibly, is whether we are dealing with a significant increase in the number of people who are trying to cheat within our sport.

On the subject of supplements, why would anybody shooting for an Olympic dream put at risk their lifelong ambition by dabbling in food supplements that have this huge, well-publicised question mark hanging over them?
It's hard to believe. Any athlete now who feels the need to take supplements has got to be certain they're clear of any suspicious ingredient. If in doubt, don't take it. At the moment a lot of athletes are taking creatine, which is allowed and no problem. But it is apparently possible that some creatine makers around the world are adding an extra ingredient, to make it more effective, without telling athletes.

If we could find the cause for this rash of positive tests and discovered it related to certain supplements, maybe we could create a category of offence called: misuse of food supplements. Everyone recognises this is significantly different from proper drug-taking and cheating.

The only analogy I can use is

that if the police come into your house and find stolen goods, you have some serious explaining to do but you are not necessarily guilty.

But there is a difference between an unscrupulous thief hiding hot televisions in your house and someone administering drugs to your body. Aren't you more likely to notice a bodily invasion? You can't be out at the time, can you?

In terms of strict liability – the notion that the athlete is responsible for whatever is found in his or her body – they have a case to answer. And I am not disagreeing with that because if the disciplinary system had to prove intent, it would be very difficult indeed. But there are supplements out there that may be inappropriately labelled or incorrectly labelled or not labelled at all. So an innocent-seeming product might actually have a banned metabolite.

Yes, but to pursue the analogy further. If your reputation and career depends upon it, why buy your TV from a dodgy trader instead of Radio Rentals?

I agree the sensible thing would be to purchase your supplements from a well recognised high street chemist. But a number of these products are provided free to athletes. Some are produced outside the UK and it's an industry without regulation. It purports to be honourable but maybe it isn't.

What we're seeing here – I sound like I'm defending the athletes and I suppose in a sense I am – is relatively low levels of metabolite. Nothing like what it used to be with oil-based steroids in the bad old days of real abuse. Anything over 2-3 nanograms is seen as an offence but, in reality, to enhance performance, it's got to be way over that.

But why is it there at all? The Nandrolone Review by UK Sport states that 'there is no direct evidence it occurs in males' but traces of its metabolic products have been found in pregnant women. Linford Christie is many things, but he is not a pregnant woman.

The evidence of certain scientists, as I understand it, states that the metabolites may be present in anybody at a very, very low level but that there may be complex reasons why this level temporarily rises in certain conditions at certain times. All we are saying is let's do the research. Let's give the scientists the opportunity to explore the supplement world. We might find there are mitigating circumstances for the positive tests. This is a grey area.

But your 'grey area' could be a cheater's haven. In a sport that is being so damaged by its drug problem why don't the administrators have the courage to be categorical? If you are over the limit – as with drunk drivers – you're banned.

Look, it's a speeding offence if you go over 70mph. But it would be seen as unfair if a person doing 71mph received the same punishment as someone doing 150mph.

It's important we know the difference between supplements which might be causing problems and the real, cynical cheating we know takes place in the world and may even take place among British athletes. We're catching people doing 72mph and we're unable to catch those doing 150mph. There are athletes in the world who we know are cheating big-time. When I was competing in the 1970s, there were athletes who were proud that they were taking steroids. It was quite open.

Foreign athletes or British athletes?

There were athletes from all over the world who used to be quite open about it. Then Britain pioneered random testing in the early 1980s but there was still a lot of cheating. Now the cheats are far more sophisticated. I'd love to think that the sport is cleaner than it used to be but I still have to recognise that there are athletes who are able to cheat by very sophisticated methods – whether it be human growth hormone or EPO – and the sadness is we're not able to catch them.

Why not pioneer blood testing in Britain?

The athletes are saying that themselves. Jason Gardener has said: 'Give us blood tests and urine tests and freeze them so that when foolproof tests are developed, you can test us retrospectively.' That is a hugely positive statement. We would like to lead the way in blood testing, but first the test has to be developed. Then you might have a situation where the suspension reflected the gravity of the crime. At the moment you get a three-month ban for too much caffeine and everything else is lumped together under 'steroid'. The word produces a very emotional response. It has connotations of the syringe, which these latest cases do not deserve.

Is it the job of British athletics officials to root out drug cheats or to protect the image of the domestic sport by getting them off on perceived technicalities?

Obviously there is a huge stigma attached to these positive tests. But we owe it both to the athletes and the sport to discover exactly what happened here. So at least we can put their test results into context.

Paul Hayward in your paper wrote something I found really offensive. He wrote of the possibility of institutionalised deceit and cover-ups. Now 'cover-up' to me implies that we throw the findings in the bin. We don't. As soon as a positive test is reported, we immediately inform all the relevant agencies. The one thing we don't do is give out the name publicly until at least the first part of the process is completed and there is a case to answer.

If there is a case to answer, an independent panel of experts are put in place to judge the case, chaired usually by a QC. It is a misconception that UK Athletics decide on guilt or otherwise. We are merely bound by the findings of that panel.

The damage done by going public is irreparable. We don't think we owe it to the public or the media to name names. If there is a case to be answered, we go public. If there isn't, if there is a genuine anomaly – like a positive test from an asthmatic's inhaler – then we don't. But the inference is that I'm defending guilty people, which I'm not.

It has been a peculiar fact of life that with every positive test comes the cry: 'I am innocent,' and fellow athletes line up with startling regularity to say: 'Oh, he/she is the very last person who would ever take drugs.' You wouldn't have to be very cynical to suspect a conspiracy of silence.

No one ever says: 'Yes, I did it.' I would prefer it if they were bold enough to admit it. I hate the fact that people's first line is always: 'I have never done anything.' Clearly, if they haven't, it's implicit in their defence. But there are occasions when people have cheated and I wish they had the courage to admit it. It's so difficult to differentiate between the honest denial and the devious denial. It's been blanket denials from the year dot and I guess it always will be.

Obviously one of the huge problems in all these cases is litigation. Doug Walker is suing UK Athletics. Diane Modahl bankrupted the BAF before that. Is government intervention required to make the rooting out of drug cheats financially viable?

At the moment, we prosecute the case and carry the liability for it. I would like to see a government-backed independent arbitration process for all sports which would carry the liability and bind the governing body to the outcome of its deliberations. This would have greater consistency and credibility. At the moment, the IAAF can overturn a guilty or innocent verdict produced in this country which, in legal terms, is called double jeopardy – being tried twice for the same thing. It virtually makes our whole process redundant.

Asking for government intervention is not an idle gesture. The integrity of sport is massively in the public interest. We're being told, 'More medals, more medals, more medals,' but we must retain integrity.

Except where is the integrity in a sport perceived as unclean?

Athletics, like all other sports, has its cheats. People are not particularly reputable in business, politics, medicine or journalism either. We're no worse and no better than any other part of society.

Last year we did 750 tests of which six were positive. We can't test for HGH or EPO (although I think it's hugely encouraging that the Australians might have come up with a test for EPO levels) but based on what we can test for, nearly 99 per cent were clean. We will never know if those 99 per cent are just taking things we can't catch or are totally clear. That's when it comes to trust. But then that's the same in any walk of life.

I can't say athletics is definitely not clean because that erodes confidence in the sport. But if I say athletics is definitely clean, that would be wishful thinking.

We'll do everything we can to make athletics as clean as possible. It's a sport I'm proud of. My son's involved in athletics and I'm delighted he is. It's as susceptible to corruption as any part of life, but no more so. We're desperate to find the truth. To say this is an in-house 'cover-up' is an insult. No way.

Nandrolone report presented

The expert committee established by UK Sport to investigate the current situation relating to nandrolone – the drug at the centre of some recent high-profile findings – has now made its findings public. The review was launched in August 1999, when UK Sport took the initiative to bring together many of the country's leading authorities in the fields of pharmacology, biochemistry, endocrinology, analytical chemistry and forensic science to conduct an intensive study of nandrolone. The group also sought contributions from other experts both within the UK and also from overseas.

The Committee's brief was to examine:
- The procedures involved in the collection, storage and analysis of urine samples, to consider whether there was a possibility of deterioration or contamination
- The various possible origins of nandrolone metabolites in urine, including dietary substances and other non-medicines
- The clarity of the regulations in respect of nandrolone and its metabolites, to consider the certainty of interpretation of analytical information.

Having had three months to conduct their investigations, the Committee concluded that:
- The collection and documentation of samples were sound and analytical methods used by IOC-accredited laboratories were reliable in determining the presence of nandrolone metabolites
- That clear guidance on the maximum level of nandrolone metabolites before a report is considered an offence, would be helpful
- The availability of nandrolone-related steroids in dietary supplements are a cause for concern
- The risk of ingesting nandrolone from food sources is negligible.

'This comprehensive review into nandrolone was the first of its kind and UK Sport was uniquely placed to lead it', said Sir Rodney Walker, UK Sport's Chairman. 'Our aim now is to make these findings available to the International Olympic Committee and International Sports Federations, as well as to the wider sports community who had concerns about the perceived confusion over nandrolone.

'The Review was never intended to examine particular cases and decisions. The Group's work has certainly provided greater guidance on the issues than has hitherto been the case. UK Sport will now be inviting the Government to consider tighter controls on the dietary supplements market to clarify the acceptability of these products for our athletes.'

Copy the French correction

By Mihir Bose

A sudden rash of nandrolone cases among one country's sportsmen is nothing new. France had a similar nandrolone outbreak in 1998 when, between September and October, there were six positive tests.

Bans quickly followed for three footballers, an Olympic judo champion and a handballer. A sixth athlete was given the benefit of the doubt because the nandrolone level was too low.

Swift retribution was possible because in France the taking of drugs in sport is a criminal act and, according to a leading French politician, that is the road Britain must take.

Gilles Smadja, France's highest-ranking sports official, talking in Montreal at an inter-governmental consultative group on anti-doping in sport, said: 'All the athletes protested their innocence but we did lots of tests and five of the six were sanctioned. It certainly helped that France has a law which makes taking drugs in sport a criminal offence.'

Smadja and the French are convinced that they have got the right solution and have observed with interest the latest British positives and protestations of innocence which followed.

A law similar to the French one may become part of the criminal justice bill now being considered by the Home Office, but Britain can certainly learn a lot from the speed of French justice.

Michelle Verroken, the head of the UK anti-doping agency, who was in Montreal, told me: 'At the moment sports bodies are taking far too long. An athlete who has failed a drug test gets a letter and it can be six or seven months before his disciplinary hearing. Sports bodies have to work with athletes. It is getting too confrontational.

'Now the moment an athlete gets a doping letter he runs to lawyers who, in trying to delay things, are asking for all sorts of details including the shoe size of the tester. It is getting ridiculous.

'The disciplinary hearing should be like a first hearing at the magistrate to consider whether there is a case to answer. You can have further investigations after that until you get to the full hearing. Because of the long gap the athlete is in limbo, the story leaks and the whole sport is like a rabbit caught in the car headlights.'

A proposal by Verroken, that a preliminary hearing should take place within four weeks of the athlete being told he has failed a drugs test, has been accepted by the governing bodies but she fears implementation may be made difficult by lawyers.

It is how governing bodies can be made to stand up to lawyers that concern the drug testers. As one official told me: 'The problem is not food supplements or how athletes are showing such high levels of nandrolone. The problem is that our governing bodies are terrified of being taken to law and made bankrupt. Unless we can solve that we will not be able to tackle the drug menace.'

The Montreal meeting was the biggest ever anti-doping gathering of sports ministers and officials.

Thirty countries were represented and all put on an impressive display of theatrics against the drugs evil – the Canadian minister went so far as to say the Olympics would 'die if the drug menace was not dealt with'.

However, behind closed doors the conference has been more about whether governments or sports bodies will control the fight against doping.

Back in Britain officials are planning to summon manufacturers of food supplements, alleged to be the source of nandrolone, to a crisis meeting next week and Sports Minister Kate Hoey is considering whether the anti-doping agency run by UK Sport should become independent.

But privately officials say none of these steps will work unless governing bodies such as UK Athletics can be injected with a shot of courage which will stop them being terrified of lawyers, echoing a call made a year ago in Lausanne by Princess Anne.

The Montreal meeting is part of the year-long war between governments and the IOC about controlling the World Anti-Doping Agency (WADA).

Both governments and the IOC accept individual sports governing bodies are not strong enough to combat drugs on their own. The IOC decided to set up WADA following the 1998 scandals when Australian customs seized drugs from Chinese swimmers arriving in the country for the world championships and French police raided cyclists taking part in the Tour de France.

In both cases the sports federations were reduced to the level of impotent bystanders.

However, by the time Juan Antonio Samaranch, the IOC president, held his world summit on drugs in Lausanne last February the IOC was so mired in the bribery scandal that Lausanne was absorbing considerable criticism itself by governments, including our own Tony Banks.

Since then a sort of cease-fire has been declared with governments working with IOC on WADA. But, as Montreal revealed, the relationship is still frosty and it was signficant that the WADA president, Dick Pound, who is also vice chairman of

the IOC, was not at the meeting despite Montreal being his home-town. He had more pressing IOC business in Sydney.

The IOC have promised to carry out some 400 out-of-competition tests between now and Sydney but many government officials in Montreal say this is not enough.

Smadja, certainly one of the real anti-doping hardliners, claimed: 'There will be 12,000 athletes taking part at the Olympics and the IOC must test all of them before they reach Sydney.'

Smadja's words will add to the pressure already on the IOC to conduct a test on EPO. Australian scientists yesterday claimed they have developed a virtually foolproof

test for the drug, a naturally occurring substance that boosts oxygen-carrying red blood cells.

The test has been developed by the Australian Institute of Sport and the Australian Sports Drug Testing Laboratory in Canberra, although IOC leaders have said it can only be used in Sydney if it is legally unassailable.

Fearful of legal wrangles, compulsory blood-testing – and even perhaps a spate of positive tests – the IOC has been steadily talking down the prospect of an EPO test being validated in time for Sydney.

Samaranch sounded less than enthusiastic when he said: 'Maybe, if we are very lucky, we will have results before the beginning of the Games.'

John Boultbee, head of the AIS, was more upbeat and said the test really could make its Olympic debut in Sydney this September. His colleague, Dr Allan Hahn, said: 'The test developed has an error rate of only one in 100,000, which should satisfy the lawyers.'

© *Telegraph Group Limited, London 2000*

Drug race 2000

Athletics' attempts to get clean before the Sydney Olympics are a sad joke, say Carl Lewis and Mark Spitz

With less than 12 months to go before the Olympic flame is lit in the new Australia Stadium, the battle to make Sydney 2000 a drug-free Games looks already lost. Though next year's host nation has led the way in developing new tests and imposing strict punishments on drug users, the mood here yesterday at the annual conference of the IAAF, athletics' world governing body, was distinctly bleak.

'The whole thing has become a sad joke and I'm afraid to say it starts at the very top,' said Carl Lewis, who was in the principality after being shortlisted for an award as athlete of the century. 'It's not just about drugs, it's about lies and federations covering up for people.'

Lewis, winner of a record total

By Duncan Mackay in Monte Carlo

of nine Olympic gold medals, believes that the main problem is that officials at the International Olympic Committee do not really want to discover a solution.

'The commitment to find a solution to the problem of drugs is just not there. There are much better ways to test than they are doing, but I don't think they truly want to catch anyone in the first place. It's terribly sad.'

Lewis's sentiments were echoed by the great swimmer Mark Spitz, whose seven golds at Munich in 1972 remain a record for a single Games. The American said that Sydney

would be 100% clean if the authorities wanted it to be. 'The IOC has the capacity and the power and the might and the knowledge and the technology to test for a plethora of drugs that they refuse to test for because of the pressures from certain countries,' he claimed.

'If, in fact, they considered the whole list of drugs for which they are capable of testing, these countries would not pass the test. It's as pure and simple as that.

'So the problem lies not in the fact that the drug testing is incapable of determining the offence, the question is, are they going to test for everything they can?

'And the answer, as I speak, is no.'

If two of the men whom many consider to be the greatest

Olympians of all time believe that drug-taking is still rife, then why should anyone else have any faith in the system?

'We have to concede that, if they really know what they are doing, an athlete can go right around the system,' said Don Catlin, whose Los Angeles laboratory handled the testing for the Atlanta Olympics.

In February it seemed the IOC was finally getting serious about eradicating the cancer of performance-enhancing drugs that is slowly eating away at the very heart of the Olympics. It pledged to take the lead in creating a multimillion-dollar independent anti-doping agency that would oversee testing worldwide and be in place in time for Sydney.

Scientists also believed they were on the verge of discovering a reliable blood test for human growth hormone and the blood booster erythropoietin, two substances top performers are widely believed to be using but which are currently undetectable by urine analysis.

These two factors, combined with the Australian government's willingness to introduce tough laws in the run-up to the Olympics which include custodial sentences for anyone caught trying to smuggle in performance-enhancing drugs, gave real reason for optimism.

Now, fast-forward nine months and what you discover is that the anti-doping agency has only just been set up amid threats from the leading countries, including Britain, not to support it, and that the scientists' search for a legally binding blood test has run aground for lack of funding.

An international conference on drugs in sports held in Australia this week has only served to deepen fears that nothing is going to change. All 26 nations represented in Sydney agreed to the setting up of an inter-government watchdog to address concerns about the World Anti-Doping Agency (WADA), which itself was set up only a week ago by the IOC in Lausanne with one of its own vice-presidents, Dick Pound, as chairman.

General Barry McCaffrey, head of drug policy at the White House, has led the concern about WADA. He questioned Pound's ability to enforce anti-doping sanctions against athletes, given the billion-dollar income that the Olympic Games generates for the IOC.

'This isn't an independent agency and I don't think anybody believes it is, either,' said McCaffrey.

It is little wonder that the IOC has lost the confidence of the rest of the world when it comes to drug testing. Of nearly 2,000 tests taken during the Atlanta Games in 1996, only two positive results were announced. That was fewer than the five positives in 1992, 10 in 1988 and 12 in 1984.

That decrease offered little satisfaction to athletes suspicious that their rivals were cheating – especially when it later emerged that five positive drug tests had not been acted upon by the IOC for reasons which were never quite clear.

Although the IOC has committed $3.5m (£2.2m) in recent years to drug research, its medical commission's chief, Prince Alexandre de Merode, said it was unlikely the 2000 Olympics would introduce mandatory blood tests for human growth hormone and erythropoietin because there could be no guarantee the tests would be reliable. 'To be fair, you can't take a medal away from someone who is tested with a method that is still not 100% accurate,' he said.

However, a panel of scientists maintains that blood testing is still possible for the Games – but only if the IOC acts immediately and puts in research funding.

Professor Peter Sonksen, whose GH2000 team at St Thomas' Hospital in London claims to have developed an effective method to detect human growth hormone, said funding was lacking to complete the project.

'We have a feasible and appropriate test for the Olympics in 2000,' said Sonksen. 'We have been twiddling our thumbs since March, the test method is up and ready, but we have seen no movement since then. It's very disappointing.'

The IOC could be forgiven for being wary of adding any fresh tests right now, though, given the growing arguments over the spate of positives for nandrolone thrown up by standard urine analysis recently.

The list of athletes to have tested positive for the controversial anabolic steroid, which already included Linford Christie and Merlene Ottey, claimed another elite victim yesterday in the shape of Germany's 1992 Olympic 5,000-metres champion Dieter Baumann, who failed an out-of-competition test. Like Christie and Ottey, both acquitted by their national federations, he is sure to challenge the result.

'After all these high-profile cases this year I am having doubts,' Marion Jones, the world's top female sprinter, said yesterday. 'I don't think I am 100% certain we have the correct testing system.'

Yet it remains the case there are still relatively few positive tests and the biggest recent drug scandals have mostly unfolded outside the lab.

It was only after French police opened the boot of a car filled with performance enhancers last year that widespread drug use on the Tour de France was revealed. In early 1998, Australian customs agents found 13 vials of human growth hormone carried by a Chinese swimmer, which led to suspensions and added weight to years of suspicion surrounding the Chinese women's swimming team.

Testing itself has uncovered relatively little wrongdoing. In the 30 years since the IOC began testing for drugs at the Olympics, only 52 athletes have been caught using banned substances. The only really big name to ever fail an Olympic drug test was the Canadian sprinter Ben Johnson, who at the 1988 Olympics was stripped of his 100-metres gold medal after testing positive for the anabolic steroid stanozolol.

Five years later he failed again and was banned for life. His chances of one final reprieve were almost certainly scuppered when it was announced this week that he had failed for a third time. Some things really do never change.

Unfortunately, if the credibility of the testing programme is ever to be restored, it will take more than just Ben Johnson being caught every few years.

Australia just says no

By Duncan Mackay

Linford Christie was just the latest victim of Australia's zero policy on doping as it gears itself up for the 2000 Sydney Olympics. The Australian government are determined to stamp out what they call 'tracksuit crime' and make the Games in September the cleanest ever. No previous Olympic host has ever made such an aggressive effort to combat the drugs menace that inevitably accompanies the Games these days.

The Australian Sports Drugs Agency will conduct 6,000 in and out-of-competition drug tests during the run-up to the Games, followed by a 1,500-test blitz which will include international athletes in-Australia in the two weeks before the Olympics. 'We're not a witch-hunting organisation, but Australia will not be a safe haven for drug cheats,' said Natalie Howson, the chief executive of ASDA.

The government-funded programme will be the largest ever conducted. The Federal Sports Minister Jackie Kelly has committed A$5 million to a strategy to clean up sport before the Olympics. The new approach has already improved border controls to stem imports of banned drugs.

Customs seizures of performance-enhancing drugs have rocketed in the past two years, prompting concerns that overseas sporting teams are stockpiling steroids in Australia in the lead-up to the Olympics. In the nine-month period up to 31 March, 1999 – the latest figures available – customs intercepted 805 batches of banned sports drugs, including DHEA (490), steroids (279) and hormones (36). The vast majority were discovered in parcel post. The figures compared favourably with 265 customs seizures of performance enhancing drugs in 1996-97 and 558 in 1997-98.

The Australian Olympic Committee anti-doping manager Craig Fleming, a former customs officer, warned authorities in 1997 of the potential for Australia to be targeted for large importations of steroids prior to the Games.

The United States recorded a significant number of steroid seizures, one case totalling more than one million doses, in the build-up to the 1996 Atlanta Games.

Athletes caught bringing illegal performance-enhancing drugs into Australia could face fines of up to A$100,000 (£39,3340) under new legislation introduced last year. The AOC had been lobbying the Federal and State governments for more than a year to amend legislation to make the illegal manufacture, import, export and trafficking of hard sports drugs subject to the same penalties as those that apply to drugs such as heroin or cocaine.

The last time a country intervened in a sporting event to this extent it nearly brought the Tour de France to the brink of collapse by revelations of widespread doping, with customs officers discovering large hauls of drugs. Kelly has warned the International Olympic Committee that there will be no hiding place for the drugs cheats. She has even promised to 'chase' every positive result to ensure that no cheat receives a medal.

> **The Australian Sports Drugs Agency will conduct 6,000 in- and out-of-competition drug tests during the run-up to the Games, followed by a 1,500-test blitz**

World Anti-Doping Agency (WADA)

Draft mission statement

General mission

The mission of the Agency shall be to promote and co-ordinate at international level the fight against doping in sport in all its forms; to this end, the Agency will co-operate with intergovernmental organisations, governments, public authorities and other public and private bodies fighting against doping in sport, inter alia, the International Olympic Committee (IOC), International Sports Federations (IF), National Olympic Committees (NOC) and the athletes.

The Agency's principal task will be to co-ordinate a comprehensive anti-doping programme at international level, laying down common, effective, minimum standards, compatible with those in internationally recognised quality standards for doping controls, particularly with regard to out-of-competition controls, and seeking equity for all athletes in all sports (including professional sports) and in all countries. Whereas priority will be given to high-level international competitive sport, the Agency will also take account of anti-doping programmes at all other levels of sport.

For these purposes, the International Federations, while preserving their autonomy and their own authority, agree to co-operate with the Agency and co-ordinate their respective anti-doping programmes with it in order to ensure that duplication is avoided and that the same application is achieved world-wide. The Agency will encourage and support the IFs in this endeavour.

The tasks of the Agency will also have consequences for anti-doping work at national level. The Agency shall co-operate with, and have recourse to the capacities of, competent national anti-doping agencies and other organisations (such as National Olympic Committees or national confederations of sport) in charge of and conducting national anti-doping work.

The Agency will help countries or federations who at present do not have effective anti-doping programmes or agencies to develop them, or, following agreement, to act on their behalf with regard to the Objects of the Agency.

In order to carry out these tasks the Agency may execute agreements between itself, the International Federations and the national anti-doping agencies or bodies, taking account of relevant international and national regulations and texts. On those occasions where there is a conflict of jurisdiction in anti-doping matters between an international and national body (or vice versa), the Agency will use its good offices to seek a satisfactory solution.

The Agency will be entitled to make proposals to the Olympic Movement and to international sports organisations and to the public authorities on measures that could be taken to ensure further harmonisation and equity in anti-doping questions.

The Agency will be entitled to give an opinion to the International Olympic Committee on the implementation by international federations of the Olympic Movement's Anti-Doping Code.

The Agency shall monitor the application of the Agency's principles and work.

Reinforcement of ethical principles and protection of the health of athletes

The mission of the Agency shall be to reinforce at international level the ethical principles for the practice of doping-free sport and to help protect the health of athletes.

The Agency shall prepare materials, aimed at athletes, coaches and others in the athlete's entourage, for strengthening the ethical principles for the practice of doping-free sport. In order to help protect the health of athletes, the Agency shall prepare similar materials for doctors working with athletes, taking account also of medical ethics.

Lists of prohibited substances and methods

The mission of the Agency shall be to establish, adapt, modify and update for all the public and private bodies concerned, inter alia the IOC, the IFs and NOCs, the list of substances and methods prohibited in the practice of sport; the Agency will publish such a list at least once a year, to come into force on 1st January each year; or at any other date fixed by the Agency if the list is modified during the course of the year.

The Agency will draw up a common list of prohibited classes of substances and prohibited methods for adoption by all sports and by all national anti-doping agencies. This list will be updated periodically, at least once a year, for entry into force as stipulated in the Statutes.

The Agency will establish a procedure for including a new prohibited substance or method when circumstances require outside the usual annual cycle (urgent procedure).

The list will be initially based on that prepared by the IOC's Medical Commission. This Commission will be entitled to provide inputs into the updating of the list, and for the identification of new doping practices and forms of use.

In order to facilitate its approval and application by national anti-doping agencies and other interested bodies, the list will be updated in consultation with appropriate international bodies including those responsible for the regulation of medicines.

The Agency will pay attention to the need to define clearly the legitimate use for genuine therapeutic purposes of substances or methods which could be in conflict with the list, and draw up guidelines for their use.

The Agency will disseminate the list as widely as possible by all available means.

Unannounced out-of-competition controls

The mission of the Agency shall be to encourage, support, co-ordinate, and when necessary undertake, in full agreement with the public and private bodies concerned, the organisation of unannounced out-of-competition testing.

The Agency will develop, on the basis of existing texts, common operating procedures with minimum, high quality standards for the conduct of unannounced out-of-competition controls.

The Agency, from the point of view of uniformity and equity in all sports and in all countries, will: determine annually the number of unannounced out-of-competition controls which it will finance; organise and conduct unannounced out-of-competition controls with the approval of and in liaison with International Federations, concentrating in the first instance on countries and sports where such controls are not at present carried out; co-ordinate and ensure harmony between such controls carried out internationally and those carried out nationally.

The focus of the controls, in the first instance, will be on those athletes eligible for, or striving to be eligible for, competition at international level.

The Agency may execute agreements for the performance of unannounced out-of-competition controls on a regular basis or for an *ad hoc* purpose. Such controls may be performed by the IFs themselves, by national federations, National Olympic Committees and/or national agencies or other specialised public or private entities.

© World Anti-Doping Agency (WADA)

UK Sport's Statement of Anti-Doping Policy

In September 1999, the UK Sports Council agreed a new set of standards for anti-doping in the UK. These new standards – 'Statement of Anti-Doping Policy' – include procedures and policies for the anti-doping programmes in the UK as well as setting requirements on governing bodies in receipt of Sports Council lottery and exchequer funding. These standards are intended to ensure that UK Sport continues to operate a rigorous and high-quality anti-doping programme, protecting athletes' rights to participate in drug-free sport as well as protect their reputation.

The Policy promotes best practice in the area of anti-doping by specifying the standards of information required to conduct an effective anti-doping programme. This includes the responsibilities of doping control officers, minimum requirements for collection procedures, the management of results and the monitoring of governing body action. Conditions regarding payment and suspension of Sports Council funding, in particular lottery funding of athletes, are also clearly stated.

All governing bodies in receipt of grant and services (both lottery and exchequer) in the UK are expected to adopt the new standards. This is subject to a three-month consultation period (from September 1999) with governing bodies regarding the implications of implementing the new policy.

© UK Sport
December, 1999

Anti-doping

Information from UK Sport

Q *Why the concern about drugs in sport?*

A Drugs and other substances are being taken not only for the purposes they were intended, but sometimes simply to attempt to enhance performance in sport. Other medications are taken for medical or social reasons. The misuse of medications puts the health of the competitor at risk. It can be dangerous. The use of some medications is illegal. It undermines the foundation of fair competition. Put simply, it is cheating.

The only legitimate use of drugs in sport is for a medically justified purpose under the supervision of a doctor. Even in this situation medicines should be sought which do not contravene the anti-doping rules and stand no risk of causing harmful effects.

Governing bodies of sport, encouraged and assisted by UK Sport, set up doping control to protect competitors from dangerous side-effects and to prevent any unfair advantage which might be gained by cheats.

Q *Are the results of my test confidential?*

A The laboratory is not given any information that would allow the identity of the competitor to be determined. The copy of the Sample Collection Form that is sent to the laboratory only has the sample numbers and declared medications on it. The laboratory analyses the sample according to the regulations of the relevant governing body and then reports its findings to the body responsible for the collection of the sample.

UK Sport's role in the management of results is to notify the relevant governing body of the results of testing as well as acting as an independent agency monitoring the governing bodies' management of drug test results. UK Sport aims to ensure that governing bodies are managing findings fairly, appropriately and according to their regulations. UK Sport will not comment to the media on individual cases.

Q *How will I know what the result of my drug test is?*

A UK Sport forwards the test results to the appropriate governing body within 14 days from when the sample was collected. Governing bodies should notify their competitors of the results of all testing conducted under their rules even if the result is negative.

Q *How can I be safe?*

A The only completely safe way is to take no drugs. Many commonly used medications, whether prescribed by a doctor or purchased at a chemist, may contain prohibited substances. If you need to take a medication ensure you check whether it contains a prohibited substance. You should not take any medication you have not checked. Remember this is your responsibility.

Your doctor or pharmacist may not be aware of the doping regulations for sport so their view on its status in sport may be incorrect. A list of examples of prohibited substances can be obtained from your governing body to show to your doctor or pharmacist. If you have any doubts contact your governing body or UK Sport for further advice.

Q *What other things, other than a positive finding, could result in a sanction?*

A What constitutes a doping offence is outlined in your governing body's anti-doping regulations. It may vary between sports but a doping offence usually includes:

- finding of a prohibited substance in a sample
- refusal to be tested
- deliberate attempt to avoid notification
- aiding, abetting or inciting another person to contravene the doping regulations of the sport (or admitting to aiding, abetting or inciting a person to contravene the regulations)
- failing to arrive for a drug test once notified of selection

- wilful interference in the drug-testing procedures
- admission of taking a prohibited substance or using a prohibited method.

If you are unsure of your sport's rules contact your governing body to obtain a copy of its regulations.

Q What sanctions are imposed for a positive drug test?

A Sanctions for positive tests may depend on several factors such as:

- the governing body regulations
- the class of substance or method found to be used
- the number of times the competitor has had a positive test
- what explanation a competitor has for the presence of the substance in the sample.

Depending on the nature of the offence, the governing body may impose sanctions ranging from a warning, to a 3-month, 2-year or 4-year ban, or even a life ban. Some governing bodies may impose financial penalties also.

Q What if I am going on holiday or overseas and will not be available for out-of-competition testing?

A If you are subject to out-of-competition testing it is your responsibility to ensure your governing body can contact you at all times. If you are going to be away from your normal home or work place such as on holiday or training overseas you should notify your governing body of this fact. You should provide them with your itinerary and contact details (address, telephone and facsimile numbers) during this period.

Failure to provide this information may be considered as a deliberate attempt to avoid testing. This may be considered the same as returning a positive test result.

Q What if I need to take a prohibited medicine for a medical condition such as asthma, hay fever or other complaints, but am still fit enough to take part?

A The doping classes are designed to deter use of drugs and methods which may enhance performance. Unfortunately some medications used in the therapeutic management of medical conditions are included in the prohibited list. There are usually suitable alternative medicines which do not contain prohibited substances. Remember to check the composition of the medicine prescribed against your sport's regulations.

If you need to take a prohibited medication for a therapeutic purpose there are two alternatives:

1. Discuss with your doctor what other alternative (and permitted) courses of treatment are available to you.
2. If no suitable alternative is available, under no circumstances would we suggest that required treatment is discontinued. If you need treatment containing a prohibited substance for a medical condition refer the issue (in confidence) to the medical officer of your governing body. Some governing bodies may agree to the temporary use of a prohibited substance if it can be shown that there is no course of treatment (that is permitted) that could adequately manage the condition. The guidelines and conditions for this vary from sport to sport.

Check your governing body's regulations to determine its guidelines for these types of situations.

Q How long do drugs stay in my system?

A This varies, depending on the drugs and the individual. Some drugs can be eliminated rapidly, while for others, traces can remain for several months.

Q Can I avoid detection?

A No – the analysis techniques are extremely sensitive; even trace amounts can be detected and identified.

Q Is it worth the risk?

A No! It may damage your health and your future in sport. In addition, it could endanger the reputation of your sport in this country and abroad.

Q Why can't I have a list of 'safe' drugs?

A No list will be complete. New medications are released constantly.

Also, the substances prohibited are subject to change. If you are unsure about a medication check with your governing body or UK Sport's Drug Information Line.

Q Why can't a definite answer be given regarding the status of herbal and nutritional supplements?

A The status of any herbal or nutritional preparation cannot be confirmed because:

1. These types of preparations are not subject to stringent regulatory and licensing requirements, therefore it is very difficult to determine whether all the constituents have been listed or whether the manufacturers would vary these without notice.
2. Some herbal preparations have been known to contain prohibited substances, in particular ephedrine (stimulant)

For these reasons competitors are always advised to take caution when considering taking such a preparation. Competitors take these substances at their own risk.

Q How much caffeine will cause me to return a positive test?

A Caffeine is prohibited when used in large quantities. Normal ingestion of products containing caffeine prior to a competition should not cause a positive result, however, as everybody is individual be aware that it could cause a positive result. Your weight, bulk, metabolic rate and what you have eaten recently has an effect on what the level in your body will be, so care is required.

To obtain a urine concentration of caffeine greater than 12 micrograms per millilitre you would need to consume approximately 3-10* cups of coffee or tea, or 9* cans of soft drink in a short period of time and then be tested soon after consuming these products.

* These are approximations only – the concentration of caffeine in the urine will depend on the amount of caffeine in the product, your weight, bulk, metabolic rate and what you have recently eaten.

© UK Sport

The control of drug abuse in sport

1. What is meant by drug abuse?
Drug abuse, or doping, is the use by, or distribution to, a sportsman or sportswoman (the competitor) of any substance defined by the govern-ing body, International Federation, or International Committee as a banned substance.

2. Why is there concern about drug abuse in sport?
It is a health risk to a sportsperson. It can be dangerous. It undermines the concept of fair play – it is cheating.

3. What is being done to control drug abuse?
The Sports Council for Wales and the governing bodies of sport work in partnership to establish a co-ordinated and secure anti drug abuse programme, whose aims are to protect athletes from the possible harmful side-effects and to prevent any unfair advantage being gained by cheating.

4. Who pays for this programme?
The Sports Council for Wales will meet 100% of the cost of agreed drug-testing programmes.

5. What does drug testing involve?
A urine sample is collected and tested for banned substances. The aim is to eradicate the abuse of drugs to enhance performance and where drugs are found, a disciplinary procedure is followed.

6. Who will be tested?
There is no way to know in advance who will be selected for testing. Selection is made at random on the day of competition or training. Some governing bodies specify that the winner in each event plus a number at random will be tested.

7. How will I know if I'm selected?
Immediately after each event, those selected for testing are approached by an official of the drug-testing team.

He/she will produce the necessary identification. If you are chosen you will have to sign a form to show that you have been notified of your selection and agreeing to attend the drug control station no later than the stated time. Usually, you will be accompanied immediately to the control station.

8. What happens if I don't turn up for testing?
Failure to report as directed will be treated in the same way as if your test had been found positive.

9. Can someone go with me to the control station?
You can ask an appropriate adult to go with you (usually the team manager or other official) but as space is limited, only one person is allowed.

10. What happens at the control station?
You will be required to identify yourself and the collection procedure will be explained. You will then be asked to:

- choose a set of 2 bottles
- provide at least 75ml of urine under supervision
- divide the urine sample between the 2 bottles or ask the Indep-dent Sampling Officer to do so
- seal the containers
- check that the numbers on the bottles and outer containers have been recorded correctly.

11. What if I can't produce the required sample?
Don't worry. Plenty of drinks will be available and you will be given plenty of time and encouragement.

12. What happens to the samples?
They are sent to the Drug Control Centre, King's College, London, for analysis.

13. What happens if no banned drugs are found?
The negative result will be reported to the governing body that requested the testing and they will inform you. The samples will then be destroyed.

14. What happens if a banned drug is found?
The positive result will be reported to the governing body and the governing body will inform you.

Usually the procedure is then as follows:

You and/or your representa-tive will be given the opportunity to have your second sample tested and should attend that test. If the 'B' sample confirms the positive result then the following course of action is taken:
- you and a representative of your choice will be able to present your case at the governing body investigation;
- a decision will then be taken. This may include suspension from competitions for a specified period or may even be a life ban;
- you are entitled to appeal against the decision.

15. What drugs are banned:
The list usually adopted is the one produced by the IOC. The main types are:
A Stimulants
B Narcotics
C Anabolic agents
D Diuretics
E Peptide hormones, mimetics and analogues

Some classes of drugs are subject to certain restrictions, e.g. alcohol, marijuana, local anaesthetics, corticosteroids and beta-blockers; check with your governing body. Doping methods are also banned, e.g. blood doping; administration of artificial oxygen carriers or plasma expanders, pharmacological, chemical and physical manipulation.

In addition, there are a number of banned drugs which are not covered by the above categories. The Sports Council for Wales will at times, hold an up-to-date list. Check before you take any medication.

16. If I am not taking drugs on the IOC list, do I need to worry?
Yes, the IOC list is not complete. Many commonly used medicines, whether prescribed by a doctor or purchased at a chemist, contain banned substances.

17. How can I be safe?
The only completely safe way is to take no drugs. If you need to take medication you should check with your GP, governing body or the Sports Council for Wales, that it does not contain a banned substance.

Remember: this is your responsibility – don't take any medication that you have not checked.

18. What if I need medicines for conditions such as asthma or hay fever or I am on the contraceptive pill?
There are usually suitable alternative products which do not contain banned substances. Your doctor will be able to advise you in the first instance, but remember it is strongly recommended that the composition of the medicines is checked against the list of banned drugs which your governing body has.

19. Why can't I have a list of 'safe' drugs?
No list will be complete. New medicines come on the market constantly. You could not rely on a 'safe' list as the list of banned substances is subject to change.

20. How long do drugs stay in my system?
This is extremely variable depending on both the drug and the individual. Some drugs can be eliminated rapidly, while for others traces may remain in the body for months.

21. Isn't it worth the risk?
No! It may damage your health, your future, the reputation of your sport and that of sport in this country.

22. What if I refuse to take the test?
Refusal to be tested will be interpreted as a positive result and there can be no second analysis or appeal as no sample has been given.

23. Could I fill the bottles with someone else's urine?
No – you will be observed at all times, even when giving the sample.

24. What if my coach or any other adviser gives me a banned drug?
Both you and the person giving you the drug will be subject to an investigation by your governing body and a decision will then be taken. This may include suspension from competitions for a specified period or a life ban.
© Sports Council for Wales/UK Sport

Testing procedures

Information from the Sports Council for Wales

The procedures for carrying out drug tests are based on guidelines from the International Olympic Committee. Therefore, any athlete tested in any part of the world should find that the procedures are exactly the same. The procedures themselves are complicated and designed to ensure the credibility of the sample, particularly that the sample relates to the individual it was taken from. This is crucial from the point of view of athletes who have often expressed concern about the progress of the sample from the site of testing to the laboratory, when obviously the sample is out of sight of the athlete. The use of individually numbered seals ensures the security of the sample as well as the fact that the sample relates to the named individual. The questions and answers below illustrate the testing process.

Who is tested?
There is no way of knowing in advance who will be chosen for testing. Selections are made at random on the date of the competition or training. Some governing bodies specify that the winner in each event plus a number at random will be tested.

What happens if someone does not turn up for testing?
Failure to report for a test is treated in the same way as if the competitor's sample had been found positive.

What happens at the control station?
The competitor is required to identify himself/herself and the collection procedure is explained. He/she is then asked to:
- choose a set of two bottles
- provide at least 75ml of urine under supervision
- divide the urine sample between the two bottles
- seal the sample bottles
- check that the numbers on the bottles and outer containers have been recorded correctly.

What happens to the samples?
They are sent to the Drug Control and Testing Centre, King's College, London, for analysis.

What happens if no banned drugs are found?

The negative result will be reported to the relevant governing body and it will inform the competitor. The samples are then destroyed.

What happens if a banned drug is found?

The positive result is reported to the governing body, which then informs the competitor.

Usually, the procedure is then as follows:

- the competitor and a representative will be given the opportunity to have the second sample tested and they may attend that test
- the athlete and a representative of their choice will be able to present their case at the governing body investigation
- a decision will then be taken. This may include suspension from competitions for a specified period or may even be a life ban
- the athlete is entitled to appeal against the decision.

The responsibility for taking action on a positive drug test lies with the governing body of sport. The Sports Councils will pass on the positive result to the governing body, which will then be expected to hold an inquiry into the reasons and take any action it feels necessary. It is the sole responsibility of the sports, therefore, to impose penalties. This is a very important principle of the drug-testing programme. It shows that the Sports Councils provide the service of drug testing and education whereas the responsibility for discipline lies firmly with the sport itself.

© Sports Council for Wales/UK Sport

Your step-by-step guide to drug testing procedures

Although doping regulations vary from sport to sport, the sample collection procedures generally follow the same basic principles and are the same for competition and out-of-competition testing. The sample collection equipment used in other countries may also vary, but will usually follow the same basic principles.

1. Notification that you have been selected for a drug test

At a competition or squad training session

In the UK, after an event or during training you will be notified in writing by a UK Sports Council Independent Sampling Officer (ISO) that you have been selected for a drug test using an official Sample Collection Form. You will be asked to sign the form to acknowledge that you have been advised of your rights and have received the notice. A copy of this notice is then given to you.

You are entitled to have a representative, of your choice, present throughout the drug-testing procedures except in the toilet during the actual passing of the sample. You may also choose an interpreter to accompany you to the Doping Control Station. With the approval of the ISO before you arrive at the Doping Control Station, you may also:

- receive medical attention if necessary
- attend a victory ceremony
- compete in further events
- warm down
- fulfil media commitments
- complete a current training session

Out of competition

With out-of-competition testing, you may be given short, or no, notice and you may initially be notified over the telephone (however you will receive your written notification at the testing session). If the ISO contacts you by telephone, he/she will need to meet you as soon as possible to collect the sample and certainly within 24 hours.

When you are notified in person that you have been selected for a drug test, a chaperone (usually the ISO) must accompany you at all times until the sample collection procedure is complete. You must stay in view of the chaperone at all times. Chaperoning is vital to ensure the integrity and validity of your sample and to exclude any suggestion of manipulation.

2. Reporting for testing

At a competition or squad training session

A chaperone will accompany you to the Doping Control Station waiting room where sealed, non-alcoholic, caffeine-free drinks should be provided by the governing body responsible for the event. If you decide to consume other drinks or food you do so at your own risk.

Out of competition

For out-of-competition testing, where no official Doping Control Station is available, the most suitable compromise is found to ensure both the privacy and integrity of the procedures.

3. Selecting a collection vessel

When you are ready to provide a urine sample, you will be asked to select a sealed sample collection vessel (from a selection of at least 3 vessels) and go to the toilet area with the ISO. The collection vessel should be kept in sight of the ISO at all times throughout the entire collection process.

4. Providing a sample under supervision

You must remove sufficient clothing so that the ISO can directly observe you providing the urine sample into the collection vessel. When you have provided the required amount of urine (usually a minimum of 75ml) you must return directly to the Doping Control Station administration room with the ISO. Only you, or someone authorised by you, may handle the sample.

5. Selecting the sampling kit
You will now be asked to select a sealed urine sampling kit (from a selection of at least 3 kits). Each kit is stored in tamper-evident packaging. You will be asked to check that the security seal is intact. If there is any evidence of tampering you should select a new urine sampling kit. Next you will be invited to break the security seal and remove the contents of the kit.

6. Dividing and sealing the sample
You will then be asked to divide your sample between the A and B bottles and to tightly seal the bottles. You will be asked to pour a minimum of 30ml into the B bottle and to seal the bottle and then to pour the remaining sample into the A bottle and seal the bottle. A few drops of urine should be left in the collection vessel to allow the ISO to test the suitability of the sample for testing.

7. Checking the seal of the bottles
Next you will be invited to check that the two bottles are tightly sealed and that there is no leakage (by inverting the bottles). The ISO also ensures that the bottles have been tightly sealed by checking the bottle tops. Some sample collection systems will require the bottles to be sealed in separate tamper-evident containers.

8. Testing the suitability of a sample for testing
The ISO will test the suitability of the sample for testing by measuring the pH and specific gravity of the sample. The pH measures the acidity/alkalinity of the sample and specific gravity ensures that the concentration of urine is not too dilute.

pH and specific gravity are measured by dipping the indicator stick into the remaining urine in the sample collection vessel and leaving it a short time. A colour reaction will occur which is then compared to the colour chart on the bottle. You can observe the colour matching process. The closest matched colour

Class	1993/94	1994/95	1995/96	1996/97	1997/98	1998/99
Summary of reports from the Testing Programme						
Stimulants	11	30	41	40	41	28
Narcotics	5	4	4	1	-	1
Anabolic agents	21	23	15	27	13	20
Diuretics	-	2	1	3	3	9
Peptide hormones and analogues	2	-	-	1	-	-
Alcohol	1	-	3	2	-	-
Marijuana	2	10	10	2	8	4
Beta-blockers	-	1	-	-	-	1
Other	-	-	-	1	-	-
Non-compliance with request for testing	6	7	15	13	14	13
No. of reports	48	77	89	90	79	76
No. of cases reported	43	68	81	79	74	73

Key: Reports – Each report is for a finding of a prohibited substance or method, or non-compliance with a request for testing. Case – Each case relates to one athlete and may contain more than one report.

Source: UK Sport

is the reading that is recorded on the Sample Collection Form.

All samples will be sent to the laboratory regardless of the pH and specific gravity reading. However, if the pH and/or specific gravity is outside the limits set by the International Olympic Committee or governing body this fact will be recorded on the Sample Collection Form. To give further assurance to the integrity of your test, a further sample is required if the first sample collected is outside the acceptable range. This provides an additional quantity of urine in the case of a first dilute sample or the opportunity for a comparative sample if the pH is outside the acceptable range. In this way the integrity of the testing procedure is maintained and claims of sample manipulation may be refuted.

Refusing to provide another sample may be considered by your governing body as a failure to comply with the request for testing and be dealt with as though the urine sample returned a positive result.

9. Recording the information
The ISO records the A and B sample numbers on the Sample Collection Form. You should check that this information is correct. You are then invited to declare any medications that you have taken during the past 7 days. Whilst you are under no obligation to make this declaration, it may be helpful in explaining a finding.

If you have any comments about the drug test you have just undertaken please ensure you record them in the comments section on the Sample Collection Form. These comments will be seen by the UK Sports Council and the governing body allowing for investigation of any concerns.

10. Certifying the information
The ISO then asks you (and your representative if present) to check all the information on the Sample Collection Form and if you are satisfied it is accurate, to sign the form. The ISO will also check and sign the form. You will be given a copy of the Sample Collection Form and you are now free to leave.

11. Transferring the samples to the laboratory
The sealed samples are placed in a security sealed transit bag and are sent to an International Olympic Committee accredited laboratory by a secure chain of custody for analysis – every step of the transfer process is documented and ensures only those authorised to handle the samples do so.

The laboratory receives the copy of the Sample Collection Form which only has details of the sample, sample numbers, and the medications declared by you. No other information is provided which might allow you to be identified. On receipt of the transit bag the laboratory staff will check for signs of tampering as well as checking that the sample numbers on the Sample Collection Form correspond to the sample(s) enclosed.

12. Reporting the result

Test result is negative

Following the laboratory analysis of the A sample, if no prohibited substances are found, a negative result will be reported to the relevant governing body or international sports federation and the B sample destroyed. This report is produced for the UK Sports Council within 10 days of the sample collection. If required, results can be made available within 24 hours during a major competition.

Initial test result is positive

If a prohibited substance is found in the A sample, the governing body or international sports federation is notified of the finding. The governing body or international sports federation, after confirming the accuracy of the documentation and supporting evidence of a contravention of its rules, then notifies you of the finding.

In the case of a finding in the A sample, the procedure is generally as follows:

1. If the governing body rules require, you may be suspended from competition and invited to explain the presence of the prohibited substance in your urine sample (if you choose to put an explanation forward at this stage). If you do not agree with the A sample finding and want to challenge the identity or integrity of the sample you are entitled to be present or represented at the analysis of the B sample. In any case this is your opportunity to formally confirm the identity of the sample and to verify the integrity of sealing.

2. If the B sample analysis confirms the findings in the A sample or you accept the A sample finding you are given an opportunity to present your case to the governing body's disciplinary panel. A decision will be made by the panel which may include suspension from competition for a given period or in some cases, a lifetime ban.

3. You are entitled to appeal against the decision reached. An appeal mechanism may exist within the governing body or at the international level (international sports federation) to whom you should register your appeal (in writing) as quickly as possible, indicating the basis for your appeal.

Refusal to provide a sample

Although these procedures have been developed to ensure security and fairness in drug testing, you can refuse to be tested. A refusal to provide a sample, however, may be considered by your governing body as though the urine sample gave a positive result. You should record your reason for refusing to provide a sample in the comments section of the Sample Collection Form and sign this form. A copy will be given to you as a record.

© UK Sport

Athletes face drugs crackdown

By Denis Campbell, Sports News Correspondent

Athletes at next year's Olympic Games face blood tests for the first time in a concerted crackdown against drugs in sport.

The move will be the most determined assault on cheating since urine analysis was introduced to detect illegal hormones in the 1970s.

The International Olympic Committee is planning to introduce blood tests at the 2000 Sydney Games in a bid to stop competitors taking EPO and human growth hormone, both of which cannot be found in urine.

Athletes in Sydney will be tested by both means as the IOC tries to turn back the tide of drugs cases which are damaging sport's reputation. Linford Christie, Britain's 100-metre Olympic gold medallist, was revealed last week to have failed two tests for the banned steroid nandrolone.

At the same time, the United Kingdom Sports Council is urging the Government to approve drastic new doping measures to check the rise of drugs in sport. They have asked Ministers to set up a powerful new doping policing agency and consider making drug taking in sport a criminal offence. 'Drug cheats defraud fellow competitors and

> *The IOC is planning to introduce blood tests at the 2000 Sydney Games in a bid to stop competitors taking EPO and human growth hormone, both of which cannot be found in urine*

spectators, and can obtain prize money when they shouldn't, so this is worth considering,' said a source.

Sports Minister Kate Hoey has agreed that UK Sport should undertake an urgent review of current doping arrangements to keep pace with the sophisticated lengths to which some athletes go to disguise their consumption of drugs.

It is not yet clear whether athletes will be blood tested on a mandatory or voluntary trial basis in Sydney. Although the IOC has been reluctant in the past to give blood tests the go-ahead, the scandal-hit body is keen to restore its reputation. It has finally decided that objections to blood testing, on practical and civil liberties grounds and from Muslim countries, can be overcome.

Next month UK Sport will approve plans to ban Lottery-funded athletes for life from receiving support grants if they commit a serious drugs offence.

Sir Rodney Walker, UK Sport's chairman, believes a new organisation is now required to test athletes, investigate cases and prosecute those found to have taken a banned substance. The sports council's ethics and anti-doping directorate could become the nucleus of the new 'justice body'.

The governing bodies of many major spectator sports back the plan. David Moorcroft, the head of UK Athletics, wants a new body independent of UK Sport to tackle athletes who resort to protracted legal action to clear their names.

Sir Rodney has also told the Government that the rise in the number of drug offenders in sport going to court may require a 'legal fighting fund' to deal with compensation actions like the £1.5 million case which cleared runner Diane Modahl, but bankrupted the British Athletics Federation.

© The Guardian
August, 1999

Anti-doping in the United Kingdom

The UK Sports Council aims to prevent doping in sport and achieve a commitment to drug-free sport and ethical sporting practices. This is a continual challenge that the UK Sports Council's Ethics and Anti-Doping Directorate meets head-on through a three-pronged approach of prevention, deterrence and education.

In practice the Directorate is responsible for the co-ordination of an effective testing programme for all sports in the UK and the conduct of a comprehensive education programme aimed at changing attitudes to drug misuse.

The Directorate also contributes to the international fight against doping in sport through its involvement in various international projects.

How is the drug-testing programme organised?

The programme of testing for each sport depends on several factors, including: the competitive calendar; the training regime; the type of activity involved; and the potential for drug misuse. For example, most sports have annual competition programmes which are well established and training schedules which support the preparation for competition. Preparation for World Championships or Olympic Games may intensify training schedules and influence the competitions in which a team or individual competitor competes.

Consequently, as the competition and training programme varies, so does the testing programme which accompanies it.

To be effective, the testing programme should encompass the major competitions as well as key selection and training sessions. This means that elite competitors will be targeted for testing, as will those nearing the elite level, either as an individual or as part of a team. The decision about the level and timing of testing is made by the UK Sports Council in consultation with the relevant governing body.

At present, testing programmes are conducted by national anti-doping organisations such as the UK Sports Council, as well as International Sports Federations. As a result, competitors training and competing in the United Kingdom and abroad may find themselves subject to several testing programmes and a greater frequency of testing. For this reason we advise all competitors to be aware of the organisations which may have authority to test them. Screening (i.e. testing of all competitors prior to a major competition to check they are negative) is not accepted by the UK Sports Council and contravenes the Code of Ethics under which the International Olympic Committee Accredited Laboratories operate.

Competition testing

Testing at competitions is generally regarded as an effective way to detect or to deter the use of short acting performance-enhancing or performance-influencing drugs, such as stimulants, beta-blockers and diuretics. However, as recent test results have shown, competitors are still prepared to use anabolic steroids in competition.

Drug testing may take place at any sporting event in the UK that is organised by a national governing body and is deemed to involve competitors of an appropriate level. Selection for testing is made from those entering a competition or named as a member of a team participating in a competition. The selection policy, usually specified by the governing body regulations, may target places, disciplines or categories as well as include a random selection. To ensure fairness the selection draw is witnessed by a representative from the UK Sports Council and usually the governing body.

In many sports such as athletics, weightlifting, swimming and cycling, a world record will not be recognised until a negative drug test has been confirmed. Some sports require a negative drug test before they will recognise an area or national record.

Out-of-competition testing

Because of the abuse of drugs to enhance training effects and subsequent performance in competition, testing in some sports has been extended to take place at any time of the year and in any location such as the competitor's home, place of training, or even overseas. Testing may also take place at national squad training sessions. Out-of-competition testing is intended to deter the use of drugs to enhance training and recovery such as anabolic androgenic steroids, other anabolic gents, peptide hormones and manipulation techniques.

The governing body of your sport provides the UK Sports Council with the contact details of competitors who are eligible for out-of-competition testing. Your governing body should inform you if you may be subject to out-of-competition testing and that you are required to keep your contact details up to date with the governing body including address, telephone numbers, place of work and training venue(s).

Competitors eligible for out-of-competition testing are usually identified in one of two ways:
- National squads/teams – all competitors named as part of the squads/teams identified by the governing body as of the appropriate level may be subject to out-of-competition testing.
- Register of eligible competitors – (usually for individual sports) a list of competitors who fall within an eligible category agreed between the governing body and the UK Sports Council. This

should include all competitors in receipt of lottery grants.

Once again, selection may be targeted towards certain groups, disciplines or rankings. A draw of names from the squad list or register provided by the governing body is conducted by the UK Sports Council who also appoint an ISO to collect the sample. Competitors may be notified of their selection for testing at any time which may not necessarily be restricted to training sessions.

© UK Sport

The fight against doping

By Juan Antonio Samaranch

The International Olympic Committee has always endeavoured to adapt, as best it can, to the constantly changing conditions of the fight against doping. Alas, the tinkerers of sports performance are forever searching to find new methods, often assisted by specialists who attach little importance to the code of ethics they are supposed to respect.

Doping is not only a danger for the health of athletes, it also constitutes a form of cheating which we cannot accept. Apparently, the desire to win at all costs drives some to turn to illegal and totally unfair means in order to ensure that the athletes in their charge gain an advantage over their rivals. As means of detection have improved, they now attempt to cheat scientifically by artificially inducing natural physiological reactions, or by attempting with various tricks to hide the evidence of these manipulations.

It will come as no surprise to anyone that, as IOC President and custodian of the entire Olympic Movement, I am taking such a serious and firm stand against these practices. Such an attitude, and such behaviour, constitute in and of themselves very serious violations of the sporting laws, prescribed in the first instance by the IOC and by a growing number of International

Sports Federations, National Olympic Committees, and indeed by governments themselves. But above all, such behaviour makes a mockery of the very essence of sport, and of the soul of what our pre-

decessors, like ourselves, consider to be sacrosanct ideals: the inner desire to surpass one's own limits, the social need to compete with others, to find one's identity within society and to develop at all levels.

Many hundreds of millions of players freely accept our principles and share our ideals, and we absolutely reject these attempts to cheat, which endanger the health and the very lives of those involved. We were the first, starting in 1968, to assume responsibility for the fight against the use of doping substances, and we intend fully to carry on, in close collaboration with the International Sports Federations, the National Olympic Committees, and inter- and non-governmental organisations.

We know that this will be a long and constantly changing battle, necessitating close co-operation among all who bear responsibility for the education and well-being of youth. For this reason, the IOC is organising, from 2 to 4 February 1999, a World Conference on Doping in Sport, so that all the parties concerned can reflect and make a firmer commitment to the fight against doping, which is poisoning the world of sport. We have already won several battles, but we have not yet won the war.

© International Olympic Committee (IOC)

Summit called over drugs crisis

Athletics leaders have called an emergency meeting as accusations of nandrolone abuse continue

By William Fotheringham

Athletics officials have called an emergency summit on Friday in Monte Carlo to discuss nandrolone as leading British sports scientists called for an inquiry into nutritional supplements and the managing director of the company at the centre of the latest case mounted a fierce defence of his products.

The 400-metre runner Mark Richardson confessed on Monday that he had tested positive for nandrolone, a banned steroid, the fourth Briton to do so in 12 months. He linked this to taking three performance-enhancing supplements – which he thought to be within the rules – in the two hours before he produced the offending urine sample.

Last night Zef Eisenberg, the managing director of Maximuscle, the Watford-based company which produces the supplements, publicly attacked Richardson.

'Maximuscle is not to blame for the situation he finds himself in,' said Eisenberg. 'His drinks have been spiked, and if that happened he is a fool for leaving his supplements lying around in the gym and at his house. Or he could be a fraud.'

In an attempt to avert such controversies, on Friday the UK Athletics chief executive David Moorcroft is likely to suggest an experiment to assess the effects of dietary supplements when he meets Lemine Diack and Arne Lunqvist, the IAAF president and vice-president, and Helmut Digel, the head of the German athletics federation.

Digel is another man with a nandrolone controversy on his hands, involving the 1992 Olympic 5,000-metres champion Dieter Baumann, who claimed a third party injected the drug into his toothpaste resulting in his positive test.

The experiment could involve the supplements being administered in a controlled manner to a group of world-class athletes, who would then have regular drug tests. If nandrolone were found in their urine, they would be immune from any sanction.

'We have to do something to sort this out,' Moorcroft said. 'The supplements athletes take are no longer regulated. It's in the interests of the IAAF to work hand-in-hand with the athletes. We can't carry on like this.'

Dr Mike Wheeler, a member of the committee appointed by UK Sport to investigate the steroid, added to the chorus of voices suggesting dietary supplements may to be blame for the recent rash of nandrolone positives: 'The most obvious reason for all these positive tests would be from the use of dietary supplements.'

He added: 'Either these are contaminated or they [the athletes] are taking supplements which they do not know contain steroids but actually do. There does not seem to be anything in this country which looks at these supplements and there should be.'

Wheeler said that tests carried out so far on supplements other than Maximuscle showed discrepancies between the advertised contents and what they actually contained. Some supplements supposed to be steroid-free did include steroids, while others contained different steroids from those advertised.

Dr Malcolm Brown, the chief medical officer for the Great Britain athletics team, called for an inquiry into the products, which are widely available over the counter and through the internet. 'People need to look at how the whole supplement industry is regulated and see if they can come up with an explanation for what's happening.'

Jonathan Edwards, the triple jump world record holder, yesterday said he considered that the runner had been 'naive'.

'I don't know if he had them tested independently,' he said. 'Maybe he did and felt they weren't a risk, but given this link between some supplements and nandrolone, it was naive of Mark to continue taking the products.'

Richardson's manager and coach Mike Whittingham added his voice to those calling for an inquiry.

'How many more athletes are going to go down before we address the issue?' he said. 'This is Olympic year and if this goes on we won't have an Olympic team left.'

Dope tests on trial

By Robert Alder

Athletics has few bigger stars than Linford Christie, Britain's 1992 100-metres Olympic champion. So when the news broke that he had tested positive for a banned anabolic steroid, the festering controversy over dope testing was bound to erupt with a vengeance.

The furore has turned the spotlight on the labs that strive to keep athletics free from illicit drugs. Athletes claim that positive results for nandrolone, the drug that Christie is alleged to have taken, can occur as a result of natural metabolites in the body or the consumption of food supplements. Anti-doping scientists, meanwhile, say their tests have been expertly calibrated to avoid such pitfalls.

But the research on which this assertion is based remains secret. And until it is published, there seems little hope that the controversy can be resolved.

'We desperately need publications on anything related to this problem,' says John Honour, an endocrinologist at University College London Hospitals.

Nandrolone is one of many synthetic anabolic steroids, which enhance muscle mass and strength, stimulate the production of red blood cells and reduce fatigue after exertion. It is prescribed legitimately to, for example, help AIDS patients maintain their weight, but has been banned for athletes for many years.

Testing for nandrolone relies upon using mass spectrometers to detect 19-norandrosterone in athletes' urine. This is the main breakdown product of nandrolone. The controversy arises because urine can naturally contain tiny quantities of 19-norandrosterone. Larger amounts may be found if an athlete has taken food supplements containing chemicals that the liver converts into the metabolite.

Because 19-norandrosterone can find its way into urine legitimately, labs accredited by the International Olympic Committee (IOC), which defines the standards for drug testing followed by most national athletics federations, have set thresholds that athletes must not exceed. If a urine sample contains more than 2 nanograms of 19-norandrosterone per millilitre, the athlete will be reported as testing positive.

But with other athletes falling foul of the nandrolone test, pressure is growing for the IOC to release the measurements it used to set the threshold for a positive result

---

Nevertheless, some athletes testing above this level have cleared their names. The Scottish sprinter Dougie Walker, European champion at 200 metres, tested positive for nandrolone in an out-of-competition test in December 1998.

He appealed and was cleared of taking drugs last month by a panel convened by UK Athletics, which governs the sport in Britain. Walker convinced the panel that he had not injected nandrolone, nor knowingly taken a food supplement containing precursors of the steroid.

Walker's lawyer, Nick Bitel, argues that far too little is known about possible sources of 19-norandrosterone for the testing labs to be so confident about their threshold. 'We were only able to find five peer-reviewed studies in the last nine years,' he says. 'We're talking about 70 subjects – tiny numbers on which to base very large conclusions.'

Honour, who acted as a scientific expert for Walker's defence team, agrees: 'I don't think that anyone at the moment could really prove that this metabolite is totally derived from a banned source.'

But the IOC says it doesn't just rely on the published studies: it has access to the test results of thousands of athletes in competition, who are presumed to be drug-free, conducted by 27 laboratories over the past ten years. 'We didn't determine the levels just like that,' says Patrick Schamasch, medical director of the IOC, based in Lausanne, Switzerland. 'A huge amount of work has been done over a long time, very carefully, by a lot of people.'

Schamasch also argues that the threshold for 19-norandrosterone has been set very conservatively, to avoid ensnaring the innocent. IOC scientists say that the normal range for the concentration of the metabolite in urine does not exceed 0.6 ng/ml. 'I think the testing is fair, it's accurate and it's reliable,' says Jordi Segura, secretary of IOC's anti-doping sub-commission, and the head of its accredited lab in Barcelona.

Whether arguments about the test threshold will be the key to Christie's defence is unclear – unconfirmed reports from Germany, where he tested positive after an indoor meeting in Dortmund on 13 February, suggest that his urine contained 200 ng/ml of 19-norandrosterone. But with other athletes falling foul of the nandrolone test, pressure is growing for the IOC to release the measurements it used to set the threshold for a positive result.

In the face of these arguments, the IOC is now showing signs of opening its testing results to public scrutiny. 'That may be one of the conclusions of our October meeting – to publish the data on which this is based,' says Schamasch. 'Now there's a need for transparency,' says Leendert Van Ginkle, head of the IOC-accredited lab in Bilthoven, the Netherlands.

But even that might not end the arguments, as the IOC's critics claim that the official anti-doping scientists have a vested interest in demonstrating that their tests are valid. 'What I'd like to see is a major independent study,' says Bitel. 'That's the only way to sort this out.'

Athletes protest as banned list grows

For many athletes, the growing number of positive dope tests is a sign that something is wrong with the testing system. They also complain that as substances are added to the banned list, athletes who have taken a previously legitimate food supplement are left open to a dope charge.

That's especially true of the anabolic steroid nandrolone. Until 31 January this year, when the International Olympic Committee (IOC) extended its banned list to close a perceived loophole, athletes were allowed to consume food supplements that contained nor-androstenedione or norandro-stenediol.

These substances can be converted by the body into 19-norandro-sterone, the main metabolite measured in the nandrolone test. And while the anti-doping scientists say that innocently taken food supplements won't cause a positive result, athletes are not reassured – particularly because estimates of how long the substance remains in the body range from two weeks to one year.

Patrick Schamasch, medical director of the IOC, agrees that more athletes are testing positive for nandrolone. But he explains it differently. Schamasch argues that since accredited labs started to use improved high-resolution mass spectrometry equipment in 1995, doping offences that in the past might have escaped detection have started coming to light.

© New Scientist, RBI Limited, August 1999

Let science reveal truth about drugs

By Paul Hayward

Let us think this through. There were 343 positive tests for nandrolone in all sports last year and every one of the alleged culprits denies abusing steroids. There are, then, two possibilities. Either they are lying as well as cheating or the tests are about as useful as a sandgrain count in a desert storm.

It brings us back to the burden of proof. In everyday life a court must establish guilt. In athletics it is for the accused to prove their innocence. It sounds sinister, Orwellian even. Yet the sport's world governing body, the IAAF, have no real choice but to stick to their policy of obliging accused athletes to explain how a banned substance came to be found in their body.

David Moorcroft, the head of UK Athletics, flew to Monaco yesterday to urge the IAAF to open an investigation into nandrolone testing. That imperious Jamaican sprinter, Merlene Ottey, calls her positive result 'a terrible mistake'. Moorcroft thinks this epidemic is 'inappropriately' undermining the sport's integrity. And Mark Richardson, the latest British athlete in the dock, argues that track and field is 'on the verge of going into disrepute'.

Fine. The right of self-defence is sacrosanct. But the IAAF have an important right and duty, too. They are entitled to challenge the implication that it is only the testers, the system, the governing body who have a problem. If the growing nandrolone crisis is all a product of some rogue element in food supplements or protein powders, let the athletes prove the link, and praise God if they do.

Confusion, panic, hysteria: nothing buries the truth so efficiently. We are not, however, facing a moral issue so much as a legal one. The positive results are not in doubt. Nor, as Richardson conceded, was the IAAF's warning to athletes not to consume exotic diet-enhancing potions.

'No top athlete even needs to take food supplements,' the head of the IAAF medical commission, Professor Arne Lunqvist, insisted at last summer's World Championships in Seville. This warning coincided with a new onslaught against doping, which the late president, Primo Nebiolo, described with a rhetorical flourish as 'a dangerous degeneracy whose damage is spiritual as well as chemical'.

Linford Christie, Ottey, Dougie Walker, Gary Cadogan, tennis player Petr Korda and World Cup-winning footballer Christophe Dugarry have all tried to tear off the cloak of guilt. This week the British Cycling Federation banned rider Phil Axe for six months after his urine sample showed traces of a nandrolone metabolite. The public are entitled to be bewildered, sceptical and astonished that simple chemical/biological issues have become so contorted.

Clarity ought to be easy to achieve. Surely Richardson has only to assemble a list of every supplement he has consumed and then have them examined, definitively, to determine whether a powder or juice can have given rise to a positive test. If a connection is found at a laboratory approved by the IAAF, they would have no alternative but to exonerate him and let him compete at the Sydney Olympics.

Nobody, though, should assume that the IAAF are on some witch-hunt, or that their drug testers are malicious or incompetent. Doping is not an imaginary problem. In Australia, incidents of steroid smuggling are up from 138 in 1997-98 to 329 in 1998-99. Science, supposedly the main hope of our age, ought to be able to shine a light into the darkness that has enveloped mankind's oldest sport.

© Telegraph Group Limited, London 2000

ADDITIONAL RESOURCES

You might like to contact the following organisations for further information. Due to the increasing cost of postage, many organisations cannot respond to enquiries unless they receive a stamped, addressed envelope.

British Olympic Association (BOA)
1 Wandsworth Plain
London, SW18 1EH
Tel: 020 8871 2677
Fax: 020 8871 9104
Web site: www.olympics.org.uk
Works to develop and protect the Olympic Movement in Great Britain and Northern Ireland in accordance with the Olympic Charter.

International Olympic Committee Medical Commission (IOC)
Chateau de Vidy
Case Postale 356
1001 Lausanne
Switzerland
Tel: 00 41 21 621 6111
Fax: 00 41 21 621 6357
Web site: www.olympic.org
The IOC is an international non-governmental non-profit organisation and the creator of the Olympic Movement.

National Coaching Foundation
114 Cardigan Road
Headingley
Leeds, LS6 3BJ
Tel: 0113 274 4802
Fax: 0113 275 5019
E-mail: info@ncf.org.uk
Web site: www.ncf.org.uk
Produces the quarterly subscription magazine *FHS*.

Sir Norman Chester Centre for Football Research
Department of Sociology
University of Leicester
University Road
Leicester, LE1 7RH
Tel: 0116 252 2741
Fax: 0116 252 2746
E-mail: jt20@le.ac.uk
Web site: www.le.ac.uk/snccfr
The Centre is funded entirely by the Football Trust and is engaged in a wide range of research projects for the football authorities and other organisations which have an interest in the game.

Sport England
16 Upper Woburn Place
London, WC1H 0QP
Tel: 020 7273 1500
Fax: 020 7383 5740
E-mail: info@english.sports.gov.uk
Web site: www.english.sports.gov.uk
Sport England's role is two-fold. Primarily, it is responsible for developing and maintaining the infrastructure of sport in England. Secondly, it is responsible for distributing National Lottery funds. In addition, it is responsible for five National Sports Centres.

Sport Scotland
Caledonia House
South Gyle
Edinburgh, EH12 9DQ
Tel: 0131 317 7200
Fax: 0131 317 7202
Web site: www.sportscotland.org.uk
Our aim is to make lasting improvements to the quality of life in Scotland by bringing sport and physical recreation, in all its forms, into the lives of everyone living in Scotland.

The Football Association (FA)
16 Lancaster Gate
London, W2 3LW
Tel: 020 7262 4542
Fax: 020 7402 0486
Web site: www.the-fa.org
The Football Association is the governing body of football in England. Formed in 1863, The F.A. is the oldest football governing body in the world. Today, it exists to develop and promote the game to men and women, boys and girls, of any race or creed, throughout the country.

The Rugby Football League
Red Hall
Red Hall Lane
Leeds, LS17 8NB
Tel: 0113 232 9111
Fax: 0113 232 3666
E-mail: rfl@rfl.uk.com
Web site: www.rfl.uk.com

The Sports Council for Wales (SCW)
Sophia Gardens
Cardiff
South Glamorgan, CF11 9SW
Tel: 029 20 300500
Fax: 029 20 300600
E-mail: scw@scw.co.uk
Web site: www.sports-council-wales.co.uk
SCW works to encourage increased participation in sport both in terms of numbers of people and their frequency of activity.

UK Athletics
Athletics House
10 Harborne Road
Edgbaston
Birmingham, B15 3AA
Tel: 0121 456 5098
Fax: 0121 456 8752
E-mail: information@ukathletics.org.uk
Web site: www.ukathletics.org
The UK Athletics organisation represents a new era for the sport and will focus on three key elements: a dedicated performance structure, a new framework for development work and a competition structure that truly meets the needs of all levels of athlete.

UK Sport
Walkden House
10 Melton Street
London, NW1 2EB
Tel: 020 7380 8000
Fax: 020 7380 8035
E-mail: info@uksport.gov.uk
Web site: www.uksport.gov.uk
UK Sport was established by Royal Charter in January 1997, to focus directly on high performance sport at the UK level, with the aim of achieving sporting excellence on the world stage.

INDEX

*****

The Internet has been likened to shopping in a supermarket without aisles. The press of a button on a Web browser can bring up thousands of sites but working your way through them to find what you want can involve long and frustrating on-line searches.

And unfortunately many sites contain inaccurate, misleading or heavily biased information. Our researchers have therefore undertaken an extensive analysis to bring you a selection of quality Web site addresses.

Australian Sports Drug Agency (ASDA)
www.asda.org.au
The Sydney Olympics has provided ASDA with the opportunity to act as a world-wide voice for issues relating to drugs in sport. This site is a must for anyone wanting up-to-date information of the subject. Included are sections on:
The history of drug use in sport
Why do athletes use drugs?
Performance enhancement
List of Prohibited Substances: banned, restricted, vitamins and supplements.
Drug Testing: an athlete's guide: drug testing, drug testing procedures, your responsibilities, your rights, positive test results, substances and methods tested for, before you take any medication.

DrugScope
www.isdd.co.uk
DrugScope has been created through the merger of the UK's foremost drug information and policy organisations: the Institute for the Study of Drug Dependence (ISDD) and the Standing Conference on Drug Abuse (SCODA) – two charities with a total of sixty years in the national

and international drugs field. The site provides objective, accurate and current information on all aspects of drug misuse for professionals, policy-makers and researchers. A useful starting point for student research on drug-related issues.

International Olympic Committee Medical Commission
www.olympic.org
Click on the No Doping link. This takes you to information on the 1999 World Conference on Doping in Sport. There is a search field here to undertake specific finds. Alternatively, go to the IOC home page and enter the word 'drugs' in the search field. This brings up IOC press releases on doping issues.

UK Sport
www.uksport.gov.uk
This site provides an overview of sport in the UK – plus a detailed look at what UK Sport is doing to help our athletes be world-beaters. If they can't tell you what you want to know then they will show you the way to get there, through the search options and links to key UK and International sporting organisations. Entering the word 'doping' in the Search field brings up 130 articles on doping-related information.

ACKNOWLEDGEMENTS

The publisher is grateful for permission to reproduce the following material.

While every care has been taken to trace and acknowledge copyright, the publisher tenders its apology for any accidental infringement or where copyright has proved untraceable. The publisher would be pleased to come to a suitable arrangement in any such case with the rightful owner.

Chapter One: The Drugs Debate

The history of drug use in sport, © Australian Sports Drugs Agency (ASDA), *Olympic Charter against Doping in Sport*, © International Olympic Committee (IOC), *Why do athletes use drugs?*, © Australian Sports Drugs Agency (ASDA), *Gender distribution of testing programme 1998/99*, © UK Sport, *What is banned?*, © Sports Council for Wales/ UK Sport, *Prohibited classes of substances*, © International Olympic Committee (IOC), *Classes of substances subject to certain restrictions*, © UK Sport, *Narcotic analgesics*, © UK Sport, *Anabolic androgenic steroids*, © UK Sport, *Why should sport be drug free?*, © UK Sport, *Drugs in sport*, © The Guardian, February 2000, *Nowhere to run*, © New Scientist, RBI Limited, 14 August 1999, *Striving for new records*, © New Scientist, RBI Limited, 14 August 1999, *Thin legal line in going for gold*, © The Guardian, August 1999, *Nandrolone, the sportman's favourite performance drug*, © The Guardian, August 1999, *What's it all about?*, © Simon Hughes, *Nandrolone crisis*, © Telegraph Group Limited, London 2000, *Nandrolone report presented*, © UK Sport, January 2000, *Copy the French correction*, © Telegraph Group Limited, London 2000, *Drug race 2000*, © The Guardian, November 1999, *Australia just says no*, © The Guardian, February 2000.

Chapter Two: Drug Testing in Sport

World Anti-Doping Agency (WADA), © World Anti-Doping Agency (WADA), *UK Sport's Statement of Anti-Doping*, © UK Sport, *Anti-doping*, © UK Sport, *The control of drug abuse in sport*, © Sports Council for Wales/UK Sport, *Testing procedures*, © Sports Council for Wales/UK Sport, *Your step-by-step guide to drug testing procedures*, © UK Sport, *Summary of reports from the Testing programme*, © UK Sport, *Athletes face drugs crackdown*, © Anti-doping in the United Kingdom, © UK Sport, *The fight against doping*, © International Olympic Committee (IOC), *Summit called over drugs crisis*, © Summit called over drugs crisis, © The Guardian, February 2000, *Dope tests on trial*, © New Scientist, RBI Limited, 14 August 1999, *Let science reveal truth about drugs*, © Telegraph Group Limited, London 2000.

Photographs and illustrations:

Pages 1, 6, 11, 23, 25, 29, 38: Pumpkin House, pages 2, 4, 8, 19, 27, 31, 37: Simon Kneebone.

Craig Donnellan
Cambridge
May, 2000

44

CONTENTS

Introduction

The Housing Crisis is the eighty-fifth volume in the **Issues** series. The aim of this series is to offer up-to-date information about important issues in our world.

The Housing Crisis looks at the housing problems faced in the UK and the solutions.

The information comes from a wide variety of sources and includes:
Government reports and statistics
Newspaper reports and features
Magazine articles and surveys
Web site material
Literature from lobby groups
and charitable organisations.

It is hoped that, as you read about the many aspects of the issues explored in this book, you will critically evaluate the information presented. It is important that you decide whether you are being presented with facts or opinions. Does the writer give a biased or an unbiased report? If an opinion is being expressed, do you agree with the writer?

The Housing Crisis offers a useful starting-point for those who need convenient access to information about the many issues involved. However, it is only a starting-point. At the back of the book is a list of organisations which you may want to contact for further information.

*****

Home truths

Information from the Town and Country Planning Association

We need more new homes

There is a serious shortage of homes across the whole of southern and eastern England.

Mainly as a result of too few homes for sale being built, prices have been forced up to unaffordable levels. It is not possible for many people on average incomes to buy even a cheaper home.

The shortage of homes for rent is causing still greater problems for people on low incomes. Housing waiting lists have lengthened, resulting in more overcrowding and sharing and more homeless families than ever in temporary accommodation.

This article has been produced by a group of well-known national organisations to put the case for building more homes. It sets out the evidence – including startling new facts on the extent of unaffordable house prices. It also gives factual answers to the arguments of those who say we do not need so many extra homes.

There is an urgent need for new homes – to make it possible for young families to buy a home, for essential workers in key public services to be able to afford somewhere to live, and for people on low incomes to have a home to rent.

What is needed now is a new partnership to meet the need for new homes which reflect the best practices in sustainable residential quality. We accept as a starting point that all new homes should be environmentally, economically, and socially sustainable and should be built to the highest possible standards of design.

We hope to promote an informed discussion on how new homes can best be provided in each district, so as to ensure the widest possible understanding and to develop

support for the most appropriate new developments.

It is becoming more widely accepted that we need more homes, provided they are well designed, in appropriate locations, and built together with the right infrastructure. However, too often the only voices which are heard when new homes are planned are those who oppose the development. The arguments *for* new homes must also be heard if the country is to meet the targets we are proposing.

The target

The target we propose is to build at least 250,000 well-designed, sustainable new homes a year for the next ten years in the areas where they are needed to tackle this crisis.

This may seem like a huge challenge for both local authorities and house builders. Yet it is less than the 300,000 a year built 50 years ago when Harold Macmillan was the Minister for Housing. It is much less than the 350,000 built in 1968 when Harold Wilson was the Prime Minister. In both of those eras the government was prepared to show its commitment to ensuring we built the homes needed to house a growing population.

Why new homes are needed

The explanation for the shortage of homes is straightforward.

The number of people needing separate homes is increasing and the number of homes being built is falling.

The future growth in the number of households

According to the latest available official government household projections, based on 1996 population data, the number of households in England is expected to rise by over 3 million over the 20 years from 2001, from just under 21 million in 2001 to 24 million in 2021. This is often described as if it is an unprecedented increase, but in fact it is no greater than the actual growth over the last 20 years.

The growth in households shows sharp regional differences, with the highest rates in the South East, Greater London, the South West, and the East of England, where the problem is already more acute. Using the most recent official figures for the period 1996-2000 (which may be subject to revision in the light of 2001 population Census results), the average annual increase in households in England was almost 200,000. This increase was mostly in the south. There was a growth of over 138,000 households in London, the South East, the South West, and the East of England, but only around 58,000 in all the other five regions together.

There are three main reasons for the growth in the number of households:

■ People are living longer

Longer life expectancy, combined with better overall health, means that more elderly people are living longer in their own homes. It is now common for people in their 80s and even 90s to remain in their homes – with support from family, neighbours, and community services.

■ More single people are living alone

More people of working age are living alone. This includes people living on their own after divorce or separation, and others not living with a partner until later in life, or not at all.

■ More people are coming from abroad

Currently, the number of people coming to live in Britain is greater than the number of people leaving. Many people coming to this country are bringing skills which are in short supply. Examples include doctors and nurses in the health service and other workers filling jobs essential for London's role as a major world city. These incomers include people seeking asylum owing to persecution and violence in their own countries, in accordance with international treaties.

The most up-to-date assessment of the need for new homes, based on an independent estimate by Alan Holmans, the foremost expert on demographic changes, who used government 2000-based population projections, is that 250,000 homes are needed every year for the next ten years to meet the demand from extra households and to take account of the backlog.

In the past the backlog has been ignored in almost all assessments of the number of homes that are needed. The 'backlog' is actually the housing crisis which we see around us. Leaving it out of the estimates of need is rather like a hospital ignoring its waiting list and only planning to carry out operations for people who become ill in the future.

In a very significant precedent the independent Inspector for the Draft London Plan has recognised the importance of including allowance for existing unmet need, and has proposed that the annual target for new homes in London be raised to 30,000 a year. It is important that all future regional planning guidance and local plans follow this example.

House prices are now so high that it is possible for a household with an income of £25,000 a year to buy a home in only ten out 212 local authority districts in the whole of southern England.

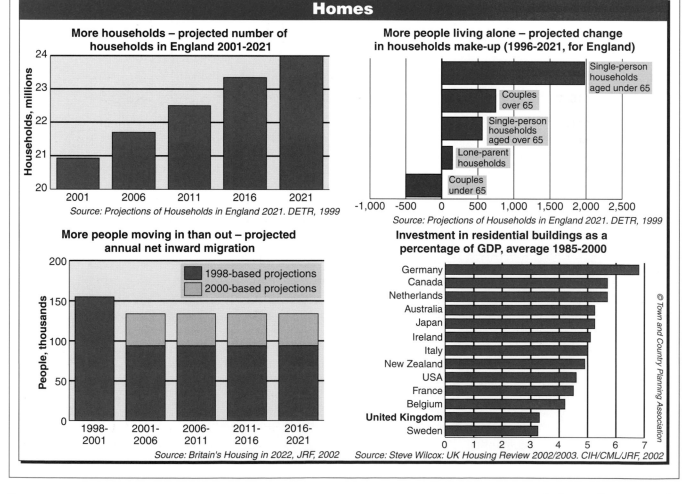

Homes

More households – projected number of households in England 2001-2021

Source: Projections of Households in England 2021. DETR, 1999

More people living alone – projected change in households make-up (1996-2021, for England)

Single-person households aged under 65
Couples over 65
Single-person households aged over 65
Lone-parent households
Couples under 65

Source: Projections of Households in England 2021. DETR, 1999

More people moving in than out – projected annual net inward migration

1998-based projections
2000-based projections

Source: Britain's Housing in 2022, JRF, 2002

Investment in residential buildings as a percentage of GDP, average 1985-2000

Germany
Canada
Netherlands
Australia
Japan
Ireland
Italy
New Zealand
USA
France
Belgium
United Kingdom
Sweden

Source: Steve Wilcox: UK Housing Review 2002/2003. CIH/CML/JRF, 2002

© Town and Country Planning Association

The shortage of affordable homes can affect anyone, even those of us who are well housed ourselves. For example, it can mean that our children who are ready to leave home cannot find anywhere they can afford, or have to move to an area where homes are less expensive.

It often means that people who have trained as health or education workers, such as teachers, nurses, or care-workers, cannot take a job in high-price areas, even though those staff are desperately needed in our schools and hospitals. It means that those who become homeless as a result of domestic violence have to spend months, and even years, in temporary accommodation.

The number of new homes being built

For 30 years from 1951 to 1981 the growth in the dwelling stock exceeded the increase in households, so that the housing shortage was reduced. By 1981 there were 700,000 more dwellings than households (although this did not allow for unfit and empty homes).

Since 1981 the growth in households has exceeded the increase in the number of dwellings, leading to a crude deficit of dwellings. Over the past decade the increase in the number of dwellings has averaged only 150,000 a year. In 2000 the number of homes built was the lowest since 1924.

The greatest reduction has been in the number of homes built for rent by social landlords. The number reached a peak of over 150,000 during the late 1960s, but has fallen dramatically since then. In recent years only 20,000 new socially rented homes a year have been built.

Investment in housing as a share of the gross domestic product in Britain is lower than in almost any other comparable advanced industrialised country.

In the Treasury's five economic tests carried out to assess potential entry into the European Monetary Union, failure of housing supply to meet the demand for new homes was identified as a major issue, contributing to excessively high house prices and economic instability.

The Home Truths project

The 'Home Truths' project is being co-ordinated by the Town and Country Planning Association, with support from the Joseph Rowntree Foundation through its 'Easing the Shortage of Housing' programme. The national organisations supporting it are the Civic Trust, the Chartered Institute of Housing, the House Builders' Federation, the National Housing Federation, the Royal Town Planning Institute, and Shelter.

■ TCPA can be contacted at the TCPA, 17 Carlton House Terrace, London SW1Y 5AS. Tel: 020 7930 8903. Fax: 020 7930 3280. E-mail: tcpa@tcpa.org.uk Web site: www.tcpa.org.uk

© Town and Country Planning Association

Where housing ladder is out of reach

Ratios of income to cost show how young workers are being priced out

A league table of the least affordable housing areas in England shows the south-west is emerging as the hardest region for young people wanting to set foot on the home ownership ladder.

Although prices remain highest in London and the south-east, the gap between prices and local incomes has become particularly problematic in the south-west, according to research 19 May 2003 from the Joseph Rowntree Foundation.

The asking price for homes in Purbeck, East Dorset, and North Cornwall demands a higher share of the typical pay packet for workers under 40 than homes in most of the London boroughs.

A study by Steve Wilcox of the University of York compared the prices of four- and five-room homes

By John Carvel

at 2002 values with the average incomes of working households for every borough and district in England. Unsurprisingly, the area with the least affordable housing was Westminster in London, where a four- or five-room starter home averaged £448,382 on the Halifax house price index and average household income was £56,625 – a ratio of 7.92.

Other areas with ratios above six were the London boroughs of Camden, Islington, Kensington and Chelsea, and Hackney. However, Prof Wilcox said he was surprised to discover that 16 areas in the south-west also featured in the top 40.

In Purbeck, the average price of a four- or five-room home was £151,386, just over a third of the Westminster price. But with average household incomes at £27,154 it had a price to income ratio of 5.58, making it the sixth least affordable area in England. Other districts with ratios above five included East Dorset, Cotswold, Torbay, North Cornwall, Salisbury, North Devon, West Dorset, Bournemouth, Poole, Torridge and Carrick.

The top 40 also included Gloucester, North Dorset, and Weymouth and Portland, with Penwith, Cornwall, in 40th place with a ratio of 4.82.

Prof Wilcox said house price to income ratios were generally higher in the south-west than in the south-east outside London. Average prices for four- and five- room homes were higher in the south-east (£152,555) than in the south-west (£124,508). But the differential between average incomes for younger working households was even wider – £38,478 in the south-east compared with £29,626 in the south-west .

The survey showed 33 local authorities where the average small home cost more than five times the average annual income of local working households with earners in their 20s and 30s. Building societies have traditionally recommended borrowing at no more than three times annual income.

Prof Wilcox prepared a second league table showing the percentage of working households under 40 in each district whose pay was too low to buy even the least expensive starter homes in the bottom quarter of the price range.

This showed 19 areas where fewer than one in five younger working households living locally could afford to get on the bottom rung of the housing ladder. Seven were in London and nine in the south-west. On this measure Purbeck was less affordable than Camden, the London borough that includes Hampstead, and Portsmouth was less affordable than Islington.

Others in the top 19 were: Westminster, Hammersmith and Fulham, North Devon, Brent, East Dorset, Runnymede, Penwith, Harrow, West Dorset, Salisbury, North Cornwall, South Hams, Bournemouth, Three Rivers in Hertfordshire and Hackney.

Prof Wilcox also calculated a key worker index, identifying local authority areas where a qualified nurse, teacher, social worker or police constable in a post for three or four years would be unable to afford the least expensive starter homes.

Even after allowing for London and south-east weightings, all but five of the 40 least affordable areas for these key workers were in London and the south-east. Four were in the eastern region, but on London's fringes – St Albans, Three Rivers, Hertsmere and Epping Forest. The fifth was East Dorset.

The 10 least accessible housing areas for key workers were the London boroughs of Kensington and Chelsea, Camden, Westminster, Hammersmith and Fulham, City of London, Islington, Richmond and Wandsworth, followed by Mole Valley in Surrey and Windsor and Maidenhead in Berkshire. The income of a nurse qualified for three or four years and working in Kensington and Chelsea would be barely a sixth of the estimated £134,700-a-year income needed to buy a typical small home in the borough. Prof Wilcox said: 'These figures provide startling evidence of how the housing affordability crisis is affecting large swathes of southern England.'

The analysis challenged the common assumption that the housing affordability crisis was confined to London and the south-east.

'When local incomes are part of the calculation and we focus on the price of starter homes it's clear that young working people in many south-western districts from Cornwall to Dorset face severe difficulties finding even a small home they can afford.'

Lord Best, director of the Joseph Rowntree Foundation, said: 'If existing home-owners living in those districts want local hospitals, care homes, schools and police stations to be properly staffed, they can no longer ignore the case for more housing.

'In the same way, families in these areas will recognise that children, once they become adults, may be forced to move away by housing shortages and unaffordable prices – or else depend heavily on funds from their parents.'

© *Guardian Newspapers Limited 2004*

Highest house prices

Authorities with the highest house prices to income ratios

Authority	Region	2002 prices for 4/5-room dwellings £	Working household incomes £	House price to income ratio
1. Westminster	Lon	448,382	56,625	7.92
2. Camden	Lon	439,968	62,061	7.09
3. Islington	Lon	329,198	47,360	6.95
4. Kensington and Chelsea	Lon	617,433	98,553	6.26
5. Hackney	Lon	203,570	34,902	5.83
6. Purbeck	SW	151,386	27,154	5.58
7. Richmond Upon Thames	Lon	303,997	54,716	5.56
8. Ealing	Lon	233,428	42,587	5.48
9. Haringey	Lon	207,884	38,153	5.45
10. East Dorset	SW	176,639	32,440	5.45
11. Hillingdon	Lon	193,556	35,681	5.42
12. Harrow	Lon	205,974	38,437	5.36
13. Epsom & Ewell	SE	203,895	38,177	5.34
14. Three Rivers	East	205,715	38,861	5.29
15. Tower Hamlets	Lon	233,415	44,260	5.27
16. Hounslow	Lon	207,868	39,512	5.26
17. Cotswold	SW	166,013	31,641	5.25
18. Southwark	Lon	202,909	38,710	5.24
19. Hertsmere	East	191,924	36,796	5.22
20. Torbay	SW	115,953	22,293	5.20
21. North Cornwall	SW	120,835	23,347	5.18
22. Salisbury	SW	152,723	29,612	5.16
23. Welwyn Hatfield	East	172,890	33,558	5.15
24. Lambeth	Lon	212,974	41,695	5.11
25. North Devon	SW	117,723	23,082	5.10
26. West Dorset	SW	139,340	27,427	5.08
27. Bournemouth	SW	145,507	28,645	5.08
28. Poole	SW	152,292	30,081	5.06
29. Brent	Lon	209,742	41,465	5.06
30. Barnet	SW	226,881	45,010	5.04
31. Torridge	Lon	107,415	21,323	5.04
32. Cambridge	East	159,048	31,608	5.03
33. Carrick	SW	123,590	24,679	5.01
34. Runnymede	SE	206,377	41,643	4.96
35. Oxford	SE	178,220	36,287	4.91
36. Gloucester	SW	128,754	26,255	4.90
37. North Dorset	SW	135,809	27,891	4.87
38. Weymouth & Portland	SW	117,926	24,245	4.86
39. South Bucks	SE	231,833	48,068	4.82
40. Penwith	SW	110,574	22,961	4.82

Source: 'Findings', Affordability differences by area for working households buying their homes, published by the Joseph Rowntree Foundation, May 2003. Reproduced with permission.

Government 'failing rural poor' on housing

By Matt Weaver

The government has been accused of failing the rural poor after figures showed that the number of new affordable homes in the countryside has halved since Labour came to power.

The Tories made the allegations after official figures showed the construction of socially rented homes had fallen to just 2,021 a year – a cut of almost 2,200 since 1997.

Countryside campaigners warned that village life was being ruined by the lack of affordable housing.

The number of new affordable homes in the countryside has halved since Labour came to power

A spokesman for the Office of the Deputy Prime Minister conceded there was a problem of affordable social housing in rural areas but insisted that more would be built in future.

A parliamentary response obtained by the Tory local government spokesman, Eric Pickles, showed that the number of homes built by social landlords in English rural authorities has fallen from 4,218 in 1997 to 2,021 in 2002.

Mr Pickles said: 'These figures show that if you live in the country and are poor, Labour really don't care about you.'

He added that the figures showed that Labour was failing to meet its manifesto pledge of providing a decent home for everyone.

Gary Rigby, policy officer for the rural affairs quango, the Countryside Agency, said: 'If we don't start building more housing for local people, then the sustainability of many rural communities will be threatened, and it will hinder local authorities' abilities to meet their obligations to house homeless families.'

He explained that the lack of cheap homes meant that people on modest incomes were being squeezed out of villages, which in turn was leading to the closure of shops and post offices.

'Villages that are dominated by second homes become dormant most of the week, making it very difficult for the people left behind to get access to services,' Mr Rigby said.

'These figures show that if you live in the country and are poor, Labour really don't care about you'

He asked: 'Do we want rural communities to be ghettos of the prosperous or do we want living vibrant communities?'

An ODPM spokesman said that demand for affordable homes in the countryside had been made worse by the introduction of the right to buy.

'We recognise there is a problem of affordable housing in rural areas and we have set targets with the housing corporation to ensure there is increasing build,' he said.

© *Guardian Newspapers Limited 2004*

Property boom squeezes out the first-time buyers

The home-owning dreams of hundreds of thousands of young adults were shattered last year by soaring house prices.

In the first 11 months of 2003, the number of first-time buyers slumped to the lowest level on record, 330,540.

That was down by close to 200,000 – almost 40 per cent – on the 526,000 sales in 2002.

According to market analysts, the trend will continue this year, sucking the lifeblood out of the property market.

Historically, the problem for first-time buyers has been most acute in London and the South-East.

However, recent price booms in other parts of the country are pushing the crisis north and west.

Figures published by the Halifax bank in January 2004 put house price rises in 2003 at 15.4 per cent, taking the UK average to £142,033, up almost £21,000 in a year.

Rises of 20 to 30 per cent were reported in the North, the Midlands and Wales, while the South experienced only single-figure increases. As a result, the average house price in 80 per cent of towns is now more than £100,000. During 2003, 88 towns crossed this threshold.

The increases have massively outstripped pay rises, which have averaged around 4 per cent, forcing those buying a first home to borrow more. Many are turning to their parents for money, while others go to lenders who have been accused of tearing up their normal rules.

As a result, it is possible for a buyer to borrow up to eight times their salary – based on a guarantee from parents – or more than 100 per cent of a property's value.

The Halifax said: 'The average house price to earnings ratio for first-time buyers during 2003 was 4.27, compared to 2.46 in 1993. The highest ratios are currently seen in Greater London (5.90), the South-East (5.15)

By Sean Poulter, Consumer Affairs Correspondent

and the South-West (4.96). The lowest ratios are in Scotland (2.92), the North (2.99) and Yorkshire and Humber (3.13).'

It added: 'Traditionally, the problems first-time buyers have experienced getting on to the housing ladder have been confined to London and the South-East.

In the first 11 months of 2003, the number of first-time buyers slumped to the lowest level on record, 330,540

'As house prices outside these two regions continue to rise significantly, the first-time buyer problem will extend into all regions of the UK by the end of 2004.'

The bank said the average deposit needed had almost quadrupled in a decade – up from £5,400 to £20,000. In London, the figure is £39,148 compared to £10,501 in the North.

Low interest rates mean that massive loans are not necessarily such a burden. Mortgage payments account for 15.9 per cent of average gross earnings, substantially lower than the 22.8 per cent in 1998 and 18 per cent in 1993.

However, even small increases in interest rates, which have been forecast for the year ahead, threaten to cripple many home-owners who are also carrying credit card and loan debts.

The Halifax said prices in the North were up 33.7 per cent in a year to an average of £103,314. This takes the increase over two years to 60 per cent. The Yorkshire and Humber region saw a 24.7 per cent rise, to an average of £97,688.

By contrast, the increase in Greater London was 8.6 per cent, taking the average to £232,421, while the rest of the South-East had a 5.8 per cent rise, putting the average house at £199,328.

The Halifax rules out a price crash this year. It said low unemployment, low interest rates and a shortage of good-quality property will underpin the market.

© *The Daily Mail January, 2004*

House price rises 2003

Region	Average price	Average increase
North	£103,314	33.7%
Yorks and the Humber	£97,688	24.7%
North West	£100,534	20.4%
East Midlands	£125,546	12.7%
West Midlands	£135,984	15.5%
East Anglia	£144,910	14.6%
South West	£160,899	6.7%
South East	£199,328	5.8%
Greater London	£232,421	8.6%
Wales	**£144,870**	**31.8%**
Northern Ireland	**£92,718**	**13.8%**
Scotland	**£84,086**	**17.1%**
UK	**£142,033**	**15.4%**

Source: House price rises – 2003. Daily Mail/Halifax

Singles now major players in housing market . . .

. . . but rising prices freezing some out

Single people have become the driving force behind the housing market in London where, in 2002, they made up over 50 per cent of buyers.

And figures published by market intelligence company Key Note suggest that the trend will be repeated throughout the UK as the number of single people continues to rise.

Single people are now the biggest borrowers when it comes to buying a home and were loaned £42.7 billion in new borrowing last year.

They make up 27 per cent of UK households, up from 18 per cent 30 years ago, but account for 40 per cent of mortgage borrowing.

The report forecasts that single people applying for mortgages will make up nearly half of the market by 2007 and also found that more than four out of five single borrowers buy on their own through choice and two in five say they value their independence.

By 2010, single-person households will predominate, accounting for almost 40 per cent of all households in the UK, according to Key Note.

However, their report points out, the rise in property prices over the last few years has made it increasingly difficult for single people to get a foothold on the housing ladder, particularly in the capital.

Key Note say that the growth in numbers of young singles is chiefly attributable to the trends towards delayed marriage and changing lifestyle and social values relating to marriage, which has seen a steady decline in popularity over the last 30 years.

In the year 2000, 34 per cent of adult men and 26 per cent of adult women in the UK were single.

In addition, the report shows that the proportion of men who are married fell from 71 per cent of the total in 1971 to 54 per cent in 2000, while the proportion of women who are married fell from 65 per cent to 52 per cent.

Over the same period, divorce increased more than eightfold for both men and women.

Despite the apparent boom in sales of homes to single people, significant obstacles are emerging for younger homebuyers.

Single people are now the biggest borrowers when it comes to buying a home and were loaned £42.7 billion in new borrowing last year

---

Figures from Key Note suggest that the average age of first-time buyers could rise to 36 years of age over the next decade, and to 40 in London as rising house prices make it increasingly difficult for younger purchasers to save for deposits.

In addition, the average deposit could rise to £32,000 by 2011. In London, that figure could rise to £34,000.

Single people are finding home purchase more problematic as prices soar and they are tending to delay purchase until well into their 30s, say Key Note.

In London, the under-25s now make up only five per cent of buyers. In 1985, almost a third were in this age group.

Now, more than half of first-time buyers are aged between 25 and 34 years old, and only 14 per cent are under 25.

Affluence, or having rich parents, meanwhile appears to be becoming a more important factor in the purchase of homes by single people. The Woolwich Building Society, for example, reported in 2002 that nearly a third of first-time buyers relied on financial help from their parents.

Faced with a property price rise of 23 per cent in 2002, young single people and first timers are linking up to make their latest buys.

A survey by the Council of Mortgage Lenders shows that the number of mortgages taken out by friends or relatives doubled between 1997 and 2001 – and last year's figure is expected to be higher.

■ The above information is from *Estate Agency News* magazine, June 2003. Visit their web site at www.estateagencynews.co.uk

The crisis of affordable housing

Information from the Town and Country Planning Association (TCPA)

The combination of too few homes being built and more people needing homes has led to an acute shortage of housing. The problems of 'affordability' can be defined in two different ways: the price of 'market housing' for people seeking to buy, and the availability of 'social housing' for those on lower incomes needing a home to rent.

As a result of the imbalance between the growth in households and the number of new homes built, there is a serious problem of affordability across southern and eastern England and some parts of the Midlands.

New research carried out for the Joseph Rowntree Foundation by Steve Wilcox (*Can Work – Can't Buy*. JRF, 2003) examines the recorded average house prices and incomes for every local authority district in England at the end of 2002. The table shows the income needed to buy a home within the lowest quartile of house prices for every local authority district in England, summarised by region. It shows the striking differences between the north and south.

A detailed study of each district shows that someone earning £25,000 a year could afford to buy a property in any district in the North East, the North West, Yorkshire and Humberside, and some districts in the West and East Midlands.

By contrast, there are only ten districts out of 212 in the whole of southern England where someone earning £25,000 a year can afford to buy. There is only one district in the whole of the South West (Plymouth), only two in the South East (Thanet and Hastings), and seven in the East of England region (Peterborough, Waveney, Fenland, and four districts in Norfolk). In London there are only three boroughs where it is possible to buy with an

income of less than £40,000 a year (Barking and Dagenham, Newham, and Greenwich).

In London the income needed to buy a property in the lower quartile of prices is over £53,000. For the South East the average annual income needed is around £40,000, for the East of England £32,000, and for the South West £32,000.

Homes for those who cannot afford to buy

The key cause of the crisis in southern England is clear. Too few homes have been built. The shortage has pushed up house prices. It is now impossible for people on average and below-average incomes to afford to buy.

The shortage of affordable homes to buy puts even more pressure on the number of people needing some form of subsidy to secure housing.

The most dramatic evidence of the housing crisis is the huge growth in the number of homeless households in temporary accommodation, which has risen from less than 5,000 in 1980 to a record number of more than 80,000 now. (See graph opposite.)

As a result of serious cuts in public funding, the fall in the number of homes being built for rent by social landlords has been still greater than the fall in the building of homes to buy. Practically no new homes are being built for rent by local councils. Compared with a total of over 150,000 homes being built for rent by local authorities and housing associations in the 1970s, in 2001 only 20,000 homes for rent were built by housing associations.

'Yes, but . . . '

What, then, of the arguments of those who say we do not need so many extra homes?

'Building more homes is self-defeating. It simply encourages more people to want a home of their own.'

It is often argued that building more

Incomes required to access home-ownership

	Average price of a home, £	Income required to purchase, £
North East	46,344	14,676
Yorkshire & Humber	52,489	16,622
North West	53,081	16,809
East Midlands	74,793	23,684
South West	100,979	31,977
East of England	102,717	32,527
South East	124,596	39,455
Greater London	169,350	53,628

House prices are based on the prices for a four-/five-room dwelling – a typical starter home – in the fourth quarter of 2002. Income required to purchase is based on a three-to-one house-price-to-income multiple.

Source: Steve Wilcox: Can Work – Can't Buy. JRF, 2003 © Town and Country Planning Association

houses is like building more motorways – which just increases the number of cars. The evidence shows this is not the case. In periods when the growth in housing has exceeded the increase in the number of households, the housing shortage has been reduced, with fewer 'concealed' households forced to share. When the growth in households has been greater than the increase in homes, the shortage has increased.

Demographic changes expert Alan Holmans has analysed the long-term trends in household formation and house-building levels and concluded that the evidence shows no support for the argument that if more homes are built this simply leads to a faster rise in new households being created: 'The increase in households can therefore be interpreted at national level as a largely autonomous influence on the demand and need for housing' (*Housing Demand and Need in England 1991-2011*. JRF, 1995).

'It is estimated that there are over 700,000 empty homes in England. We should be using these instead of building more.'
More should be done to bring into use homes that are empty without good reason, using the policies advocated by the Empty Homes Agency. The first target should be to bring back into use properties that have been empty for six months or more, and compulsory powers should be used where these are necessary to bring homes back into use.

However, it is widely accepted that a 'vacancy rate' of 3 per cent in the housing stock is needed to allow for properties to be renovated and for gaps between people moving out and new occupiers moving in. With a total housing stock of over 20 million, this means that at any time 600,000 homes may be empty. A reduction in the number of empty homes is required, but is not an absolute alternative to building new homes.

'The projections of the need for new homes may be wrong, as they have been in the past.'
Projections of population, household growth, and migration have some-

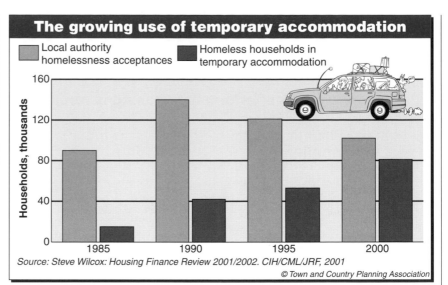

The growing use of temporary accommodation

Local authority homelessness acceptances

Homeless households in temporary accommodation

Households, thousands

Source: Steve Wilcox: Housing Finance Review 2001/2002. CIH/CML/JRF, 2001
© Town and Country Planning Association

times been inaccurate in the past – but mostly because they have been too low, not too high. The 2001 Census indicates that the growth in households may have been less than expected. Estimates of the requirement for new homes over the next 20 years can be revised if experience shows this to be appropriate, but on current projections there is a huge gap between potential requirement and current supply. The indisputable fact is that house-building over the past ten years has failed to match the growth in households, and that as a result there is a severe shortage of housing across the whole of southern England. The key issue is what is done now.

'There is no more land left to build on.'
A Government study in 1995 showed that the urban area of England was 10.6 per cent and would increase to 11.9 per cent by 2016. Areas of outstanding natural beauty make up 16 per cent of the countryside, 12 per cent is designated as green belt land, and 8 per cent is covered by national parks. The growth in the productivity of agriculture and the increasing share of food imported from abroad have reduced the requirement for agricultural land.

The green belt has played a valuable role in restricting outward expansion into the countryside. However, greenfield sites in southern England include a significant amount of low-quality land with little useful agricultural, recreational, or environmental purpose. There is still significant scope for building new

homes, provided they are built in the most appropriate areas.

'We should be building homes on brownfield sites in the cities.'
Government policy and planning guidance now requires a 'sequential approach', through which building should only take place on greenfield land where it is not possible to build on brownfield land. It is accepted that up to 40 per cent of new homes will have to be built on greenfield land. Following the report of the Urban Task Force and the Government's Urban White Paper, all local authorities have been urged to take all possible steps to achieve sustainable regeneration.

The Mayor's Plan for London provides an example of how this new approach is being put into practice, with policies for increasing densities for new house-building, and development of unused and derelict land, especially in the Thames Gateway. However, a significant number of the potential sites suffer from serious contamination, poor access to transport links, or low environmental quality, such as overhead pylons, close proximity to heavily used traffic routes, or noisy commercial activity.

The evidence shows that the need is to build on all feasible brownfield sites and to apply the higher densities sought by the Government and to make best use of under-used resources outside the southern part of the country but still to build on greenfield land in southern England.

© *Town and Country Planning Association (TCPA)*

Tipping the balance

How a lack of affordable housing is forcing Londoners into poverty

London's housing is the most expensive in the country. It is making its people some of the poorest.

Wherever they live, people are more likely to experience poverty once their housing costs are taken into account. But in London the difference between the number of people in poverty before and after housing costs are taken into account is much greater than in other areas of the country. After housing costs, Inner London has a far higher instance of poverty for children, working-age adults and pensioners than any region or country in Great Britain.

Poverty and equality

Children in poverty
- Before housing costs, 25% of children are in poverty in Greater London. The national average is 21%.
- After housing costs, 41% of children are in poverty in Greater London, this rises to 53% in Inner London. The national average is 30%.
- After housing costs, 73% of London's Pakistani and Bangladeshi children and 55% of London's black children are living in poverty.

Working-age adults in poverty
- Before housing costs, 15% of working-age adults are in poverty in Greater London. This compares with East and South East England, which have 9% and 8% respectively.
- After housing costs, 23% of working-age adults are in poverty in Greater London, rising to 30% in Inner London. This compares with East and South East England, which have 14% and 13% respectively.
- After housing costs, 63% of single working-age adults with children are in poverty in Greater London.

Pensioners in poverty
- Before housing costs, 17% of pensioners are in poverty in

Greater London. The national average is 22%.
- After housing costs, 26% of pensioners are in poverty in Greater London, rising to 36% in Inner London. The national average is 25%.

The lack of affordable housing is not only forcing Londoners into poverty, it is resulting in thousands living in overcrowded, unsuitable homes. This has a direct impact on Londoners' health and the educational achievement of London's children.

The average cost of buying a home in London is £228,625 compared to a national average of £140,624

London is paying a high price for under-investment in affordable housing and spiralling house prices.

All of the above figures are from *London Divided: Income Equality and Poverty in the Capital*, GLA, November 2002. Poverty is defined as 60% of the national median disposable household income.

Buying and earnings

An expensive private sector
56% of London households are owner-occupiers (Census 2001). However, with increasing property prices this is an option that is becoming increasingly difficult for working Londoners.
- The average cost of buying a home in London is £228,625 compared to a national average of £140,624.

- The average cost of renting a home in London is £280 a week (£14,560 a year).
- To buy an average-priced home in London would require a single gross salary of over £62,055. The average annual London salary is £32,448.
- The average gross income of a nurse in London is £24,000, whilst a postal worker can expect to earn £18,000 a year, a secretary or PA will earn on average £21,600 and a sales assistant can only expect to earn £12,800 a year (figures based on weekly (x 48) New Earnings Survey, ONS, 2002).
- The average net weekly income of workers in London is £403. Renting an average-priced one-bedroom home would take 51% of an average worker's income. If that worker had a family and needed to rent a three-bedroom flat it would take 72% of their net weekly income.
- Last year the average deposit put down by first-time buyers in London was £41,663. This is nearly two and a half times the national average deposit (£18,262) and almost £10,000 more than the average annual London income (Halifax House Price Index, March 2003).
- The average shared-ownership home sold by a housing association during 2001/02 was 66% of the cost of buying the same property outright. For thousands of working Londoners low-cost home-ownership schemes are the only solution to meet their aspirations for home ownership and therefore enable them to continue to live and work in the capital.

Supply and demand

A shortage of affordable housing
Despite increasing demand for affordable housing and increased government investment, the total

number of homes available for social renting continues to fall.

- Since the introduction of the Right To Buy, over 250,000 social rented homes have been sold in London (Right To Buy data, ODPM, 2002).
- The number of households on local authority housing registers in London rose by 7% in a year to over 226,000 households (ODPM, Housing Investment Programme, 2002).
- In 2000/01, across all sectors, a total of 14,205 new homes were completed in London (ODPM, 2000/01).
- Last year government funding of housing associations through the Housing Corporation resulted in 6,289 additional affordable homes in London. Of these 3,344 were newly built for affordable rent (Housing Corporation Completions, April 2001-March 2002).
- An estimated 50% of new households will not have the income needed to become owner-occupiers and will need subsidised housing (London Regional Housing Statement 1999, Housing Corporation & Government Office for London).
- London has a severe shortage of large affordable homes. 12,000 homes, with five or more bedrooms, are needed just by housing associations for tenants who are currently living in overcrowded accommodation (LHF analysis of housing association transfer lists as of August 2002).
- In 2001/02 1,165 shared-ownership homes were completed by housing associations (Housing Corporation Completions, April 2001-March 2002). During the same period London's largest providers of shared ownership received over 120,000 enquiries about the scheme and more than 34,000 completed applications (London Home Ownership Group benchmarking exercise, 2002).

An increase in homelessness

With the private sector out of reach and huge competition for affordable housing, homelessness in the capital is at an all-time high.

- In 2001/02 London's local authorities accepted responsibility for 28,652 homeless households (ODPM, Housing Investment Programme, 2002).
- 57,466 households are in temporary accommodation in London. This compares with 48,700 in November 2000 (GLA Homelessness Bulletin 41, December 2002).
- Of those in temporary accommodation, more than 8,000 households are in Bed and Breakfast accommodation or shared annexes (GLA Homelessness Bulletin 41, December 2002).

Bed & breakfast

- 53% of the households in Bed and Breakfast or shared hotel annexes in London are families with children or pregnant women and, of these, an estimated 78% have lived in this type of accommodation for more than six weeks (GLA Homelessness Bulletin 41, December 2002).
- An estimated average of 348 people sleep rough on London's streets each night (ODPM, Housing Investment Programme, 2001-02).
- London local authorities spent a total of £132 million on homelessness in 2001/02 (CIPFA, 2001/02).

The cost of buying in the private sector

Borough	Cost of average home[1]	Gross annual income needed for mortage[2]	Average gross income for full time employee in borough[3]
Barking & Dagenham	£117,672	£31,939	£26,260
Barnet	£259,600	£70,463	£27,404
Bexley	£150,520	£40,855	£23,192
Brent	£209,599	£56,891	£24,024
Bromley	£209,844	£56,958	£20,904
Camden	£382,999	£103,957	£34,164
City of London	£268,988	£73,011	£50,544
City of Westminster	£447,399	£121,437	£37,232
Croydon	£164,885	£44,755	£25,324
Ealing	£215,851	£58,588	£27,248
Enfield	£207,592	£56,346	£25,740
Greenwich	£164,104	£44,542	£23,972
Hackney	£216,789	£58,843	£32,292
Hammersmith & Fulham	£309,274	£83,946	£32,188
Haringey	£218,721	£59,367	£22,724
Harrow	£208,674	£56,640	£26,156
Havering	£158,926	£43,137	£19,656
Hillingdon	£178,069	£48,333	£27,872
Hounslow	£214,010	£58,088	£30,212
Islington	£241,441	£65,534	£34,476
Kensington & Chelsea	£568,265	£154,243	£30,940
Kingston Upon Thames	£202,845	£55,058	£27,508
Lambeth	£217,441	£59,020	£30,004
Lewisham	£161,189	£43,751	£24,752
Merton	£225,447	£61,193	-------
Newham	£134,708	£35,564	£24,336
Redbridge	£183,908	£49,918	£24,856
Richmond Upon Thames	£315,682	£85,685	-------
Southwark	£191,350	£51,938	£32,448
Sutton	£185,454	£50,337	£25,480
Tower Hamlets	£208,402	£56,566	£40,196
Waltham Forest	£142,786	£38,756	£24,336
Wandsworth	£262,183	£71,164	£26,884
Great London Average	**£228,625**	**£62,055**	**£32,448**

1 Land Registry, January-December 2002
2 NHF Research based on 95% mortgage, 3.5 x salary.
3 New Earnings Survey, April 2002.
----- Not recorded.

Source: 'Tipping the Balance', London Housing Federation 2003

Overcrowding and poor housing conditions

High housing costs not only make Londoners poor, they also mean that many people cannot afford the size of home they need or a home that is in a reasonable state of repair.

- All 10 of the country's local authority areas with most over-crowded households are in London (Census 2001).
- An average of 17% of all households in London boroughs are overcrowded (Census 2001).
- 8% of all households in London do not have central heating (Census 2001).
- Almost 8% of London's households cannot afford to heat their homes to the standard they require (GLA, 2002 Household survey).
- 7% of all homes in London are recorded as unfit dwellings. Of these 13% belong to local authorities and 3% belong to housing associations who require further funding to bring them back into use (ODPM, Housing Investment Programme 2002).
- London's housing is old. 60% of dwellings were built before 1944 whereas only 34% of dwellings in England overall were built before this date (DTLR, English House Condition Survey 1996).

Redressing the balance: increasing housing choice for Londoners

If we are to stop housing costs being a major cause of poverty amongst Londoners, the supply of affordable housing needs to be dramatically increased. The capital's fast growing population means that the situation will only get worse if there is no immediate action to redress the balance.

An equally important challenge is to ensure that the mistakes of the past are not repeated and soulless, isolated estates built. The new affordable homes created must be popular, thriving, well-connected places where people choose to live.

The Government is now recognising the scale of London's housing problems and the effect they are having on the capital both in terms of homelessness and difficulties in

recruiting and retaining staff. Increased investment and a commitment to building sustainable communities is a welcome start. But there is a lot to be achieved before the cost of housing no longer drives people from the capital or forces them into poverty.

We need:

- An increase, year on year, in the overall level of government resources for affordable homes across the capital.
- A London-wide average of 50% of all new housing to be affordable homes.
- Housing associations to be given support to develop a wide range of affordable housing options that meet Londoners' aspirations. These should include both rented and home-ownership solutions.
- Both public and private sector employers to recognise the role they can play in helping house London's workers through partnerships with housing associations.
- An efficient planning system which is a catalyst rather than a barrier to development.
- Planners of higher density housing developments to consider social as well as physical sustainability.
- A real choice for residents of affordable housing in terms of the location, type and tenure of their home.
- More incentives for people to move from under-occupied large homes.
- Innovative and creative approaches to making the best use of empty homes, commercial buildings and government-owned buildings.

The London Housing Federation

The London Housing Federation is a regional office of the National Housing Federation, the trade body representing housing associations throughout the country. The London Housing Federation campaigns for and promotes better homes for Londoners.

The London Housing Federation represents the views of member organisations by taking a lead role in housing debates, consultations, discussions and steering groups on issues relevant to housing. We meet regularly and work in partnership with the London region of the Housing Corporation, Greater London Authority, Government Office for London, the Association of London Government and others. Together, we proactively address issues through the Housing Forum for London and the London Housing Strategy.

Our 450 members, London's Housing Associations, are not-for-profit organisations which provide affordable housing for Londoners in housing need. These range from homeless families to elderly people requiring supported housing and workers on moderate incomes who are struggling to live and work in the capital. Housing associations actively contribute to neighbourhoods, not only providing housing but also a range of other services.

- This article was produced by the London Housing Federation and written by Laura Hare, Lisa Wimborne and Anna Hollis. Thanks to the National Housing Federation Resource, Research and Information Department, Zoe Belcher and Chris Smith at the Greater London Authority. For further information about the work of the London Housing Federation log on to www.housing.org.uk/london

The figures provided in this document are the recorded figures from sources quoted. In some instances the sources do not include figures from all of the 33 London boroughs. In these cases, estimates may have been made of a London total.

London's housing crisis

Facts and figures

Affordable housing: supply and demand

- The number of households in London is likely to grow in the coming years, meaning that demand for affordable housing in London will only increase.
- Currently, there is not enough affordable housing being constructed to adequately address this demand.
- The supply of new housing over the past 20 years has averaged about 20,000 units per annum, but only a small percentage is estimated to be affordable. The Mayor estimates that 31,900 new homes are needed each year, 50 per cent of which should be affordable.
- The number of new lettings made by councils and housing associations has fallen by 26 per cent over the last five years.

Prices

- House prices in London are 1.6 times the average for England and Wales. A first-time buyer pays on average £193,508 for a home in London, nearly double the UK average of £103,294 (July 2003).
- Average private sector rents are more than three times the UK average.

Empty homes

- There are nearly 100,000 empty homes in London, 83 per cent of which are in the private sector (April 2002).
- 41,000 private homes have been empty for more than six months (April 2002).

Inappropriate and poor-quality accommodation

- Around 31,000 households were accepted as homeless by London's local authorities between April 2002 and April 2003.

House prices in London are 1.6 times the average for England and Wales. A first-time buyer pays on average £193,508 for a home in London, nearly double the UK average of £103,294

- Over 61,000 homeless households in London have been placed in temporary accommodation by London borough housing departments (July 2003).
- Around 14,000 single homeless Londoners are living in hostels (March 2003).

- Approximately 320 people are sleeping on the streets of London (June 2002).
- Seven per cent of London's housing stock is deemed unfit (April 2002).

Asylum seekers

- 18,500 asylum-seeking households are supported by London social services departments (August 2003);
- An additional 37,000 are supported by the National Asylum Support Service (March 2003).

Public opinion

- In the Mayor's 2002 annual opinion survey of Londoners, the cost of housing was ranked among the top three worst things about London, while over half of those surveyed thought that affordable housing and property prices should be one of the top priorities for improving London as a place to live.
- The Prime Minister's strategy unit found in a report (2003) that housing was one of the top two reasons people leave London.

- The above information is from the Mayor of London's web site which can be found at www.london.gov.uk

© *Greater London Authority 2004*

Housing and the environment

Information from renewal.net

Overview

Poor standards of housing and the environment exert a major influence over a range of other issues affecting disadvantaged neighbourhoods. Substandard stock jeopardises health, poor design encourages crime, and where neighbourhoods appear run-down and neglected it reinforces negative attitudes, undermines local confidence and reinforces unpopularity and low demand. Strategies need to address issues of tenure and wider neighbourhood management, as well as the quality of the stock and standards of housing management.

Most of the neighbourhoods prioritised by the national strategy display inadequate standards of housing, and poorly planned and often degraded environments.

What's the problem?

Alongside high levels of crime and worklessness, and poor standards of health and education, most of the neighbourhoods on which the national strategy focuses also display inadequate standards of housing, and poorly planned and often degraded environments. In both cases, a derelict physical environment can contribute to a range of other issues affecting disadvantaged neighbourhoods, for example by:

- contributing to a neighbourhood's poor reputation, and thus 'sustaining its unpopularity'
- reducing demand for housing in the area and
- undermining local residents' confidence and self-esteem.

But the relationship between housing and neighbourhood renewal extends beyond the physical condition of the housing stock. Critical issues that neighbourhood renewal partnerships need to consider in developing strategies for housing and the environment include:

- The relationship between tenure mix and the stability of population within neighbourhoods: tenure diversification (through the introduction of higher levels of owner occupation) is often seen as a way of stabilising populations by increasing residents' stake in the area;
- The impact of housing design on patterns and types of crime;

Poor standards of housing and the environment exert a major influence over a range of other issues affecting disadvantaged neighbourhoods

---

- The consequences of substandard physical conditions for health, and of overcrowding for educational attainment;

- The impact of standards of housing management – often remote and unresponsive – on resident satisfaction;
- The relationship between neighbourhood (and indeed local authority district) housing strategies and the wider housing market.

What's the explanation?

A variety of issues combine to create that combination of neglect, unpopularity, stigma and disadvantage that are present in many neighbourhood renewal areas. Some of the more obvious include:

- Underinvestment in and neglect of the physical stock – which includes inadequate maintenance of social housing stock, and lack of upkeep by private landlords and homeowners;
- Poor design: very often the lack of maintenance may have compounded initial design faults and low building standards;
- Changes in the surrounding economic context: job losses in

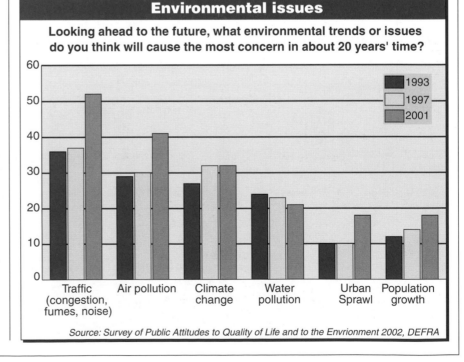

Environmental issues

Looking ahead to the future, what environmental trends or issues do you think will cause the most concern in about 20 years' time?

Legend: 1993, 1997, 2001

Categories: Traffic (congestion, fumes, noise); Air pollution; Climate change; Water pollution; Urban Sprawl; Population growth

Source: Survey of Public Attitudes to Quality of Life and to the Environment 2002, DEFRA

the surrounding area, which means the most employable leave in search of jobs elsewhere, replaced by those already on benefit – leading to empty properties and the start of a downward spiral.

But two other factors are crucial to the creation and maintenance of this spiral:

- The way the benefit system and local housing allocation policies combine to concentrate and lock poor people in decaying neighbourhoods;
- Changes in patterns of demand for social housing. Not all neighbourhood renewal areas are dominated by social housing, but where they are, they are threatened by the growing unpopularity of social housing, and the fact that for many, it's seen as a stepping stone to owner occupation. New households seeking social housing are likely to be in less secure employment than in the past, adding to the increasing volatility of the housing market. The relatively large numbers of elderly people living in social housing will lead to an increased flow of social housing properties in the next few years – with the risk of a further increase in neighbourhood instability.

What's the policy context?

The current housing policy framework was set out in a policy statement at the end of 2000, which followed a period of consultation on an earlier Green Paper. The broad thrust of the policy statement is encapsulated in the objectives of the DTLR housing directorate, which are:

- 'To assist Ministers in meeting the aim of offering everyone the opportunity of a decent home and so promote social cohesion, well-being and self-dependence.'

Some of the specific dimensions of the policy of most immediate relevance to neighbourhood renewal include:

- Raising the quality of social housing;
- New affordable housing;
- Creating new forms of tenure;
- Tackling other forms of social exclusion such as: rough sleepers; supporting people, to assist vulnerable tenants in sheltered and supported housing, tackling fuel poverty, improving travellers' sites; and dealing with anti-social behaviour.

Under the national strategy, Local Authorities and Registered Social Landlords are set the target of ensuring that all social housing meets set standards of decency by 2010, reducing the number of households living in social housing that do not meet these targets by one-third between 2001 and 2004. The standard is defined in relation to the physical quality of the housing (for example, the physical condition, amenities, quality of insulation and so on).

References:

Cole I., *National Evaluation of New Deal for Communities: Housing and Physical Environment Domain: Review of the Evidence Base* (Centre for Regional Economic and Social Research, Sheffield Hallam University)

DETR, *Housing Policy Statement: The Way Forward for Housing* (DTLR, 2000)

DETR, *Quality and Choice – a decent home for all* (DETR, 2000)

Evans R., Fordham G., *Regeneration that lasts: A Guide to Good Practice on Social Housing Estates* (DETR, 2000)

Maclennan D., *Changing places, engaging people* (JRF, 2000)

Murie A., *Changing demand and Unpopular Housing* (Housing Corporation, 1998)

Policy Action Team 5: Housing Management (Cabinet Office, 2000)

- The above information is from renewal.net's web site which can be found at www.renewal.net

© Crown copyright

Brownfield? Greenfield?

The threat to London's unofficial countryside

Brownfield or greenfield?

London has the chance of a brighter future. Central government is committed to an urban renaissance to create vibrant liveable cities. At the same time, London's regional government, the Greater London Authority, has the opportunity of working on behalf of the whole city.

London Wildlife Trust believes that any talk of urban renaissance must recognise the value of natural areas that already exist. A significant element of the Government's proposals is the prioritisation of brownfield sites for development. By 2008, 60% of new housing should either be built on brownfield sites or created from property conversions. Yet, about a quarter of London's 1,200 wildlife sites[1] are wholly or partly brownfield in character. And seven of inner London's Sites of Metropolitan Importance,[2] which were designated for their wasteland biodiversity, have now been destroyed or so damaged that they no longer merit such wildlife status. London's remaining brownfield sites with the most valuable wildlife must be saved.

The Government's brownfield targets accentuate the 'brownfield versus greenfield' debate. This tends to focus on meeting house-building targets, protecting the greenbelt and preventing urban sprawl. Yet, much of our countryside has been polluted and damaged by industrialised farming methods. In many areas, such as rural Essex, the countryside is dominated by endless tracts of featureless prairies. These are technically green fields but they are often sterile areas for people and wildlife. Similarly, our greenbelt land, strongly protected against development by planning policy, is often inappropriately managed and of low wildlife, landscape and recreational value.

In contrast, urban brownfields can be very rich in wildlife, providing a refuge for many plants and wild animals. These colourful wasteland

communities, that spring up spontaneously wherever land is abandoned, are one of the few remaining truly natural types of habitat in the country. The contrast of natural and industrial heritage can be strikingly attractive and interesting. But the opportunities it offers for recreation are often ignored.

Not all brownfield sites have a high wildlife and amenity value. Certain sites, such as areas of hard-standing, car parks and existing empty buildings, should be targeted for redevelopment first. In other cases, creative mitigation can allow redevelopment to go ahead without the destruction of local wildlife characteristics. We need to recognise the potential contribution of these sites in areas with very limited natural open space.

Natural redevelopment

Wastelands have always had a chequered history. They appeared because of accident, politics or economic failure and often disappeared just as unexpectedly. But today, more wastelands are being lost to development than are being created. And this means that the unique wildlife features of some of our existing sites are even more precious.

The illustration below indicates how the process of natural colonisation can work on brownfields. It shows that wasteland or brownfield habitat can be very varied: from sparsely vegetated ground to areas of relatively mature trees and shrubs. In this article, brownfield biodiversity refers to all of these types.

Substrate conditions and the level of human activity strongly influence the pattern of colonisation. On larger brownfield sites there may be a variety of wildlife communities at different stages of natural colonisation.

This can result in an amazing array of plant-life, which in turn encourages foraging and nesting birds, including linnet, goldfinch, skylark, song thrush and kestrel. In London, these dynamic landscapes have also attracted a rare bird in the UK, the black redstart. Other animals that make use of urban wastelands include foxes and bats, as well as butterflies, grasshoppers and slow-worm.

The diverse origins of urban brownfields can result in wildlife species that would be the envy of many rural nature reserves. Certain

bare ground · sparce cover of pioneer plants · herbs, grasses and bienel plants · patches of scrubby bushes · young woodland

nationally-important invertebrates, such as the 'humble bumble', *Bombus humilis*, are virtually restricted in London to a mosaic of brownfield and relic grassland sites in the East Thames corridor. These places offer the unusual, but essential, combination in the city of sandy or stone substrates and an abundance of nectar-rich wildflowers.

Wastelands are also unique in the way their species reflect our history and cultural diversity. For example, plants and animals, imported into our cities from around the world, colonised wasteland sites around ports. London's docklands, once the hub of trading activity, provided a home for many wildlife stowaways. Railway yards and container parks continue to do so today. As a result, there is a great variation between species found on wasteland sites across London and other parts of the country.

Natural space for people

There is increasing evidence that we benefit from contact with nature as part of our everyday lives. Easy access to natural green space makes us feel better, both physically and mentally.

These benefits have been acknowledged by the London Mayor, who proposes in his Biodiversity Strategy that all Londoners, wherever they live or work, should be within walking distance of a quality natural space. In many built-up areas, particularly in inner London, wastelands and other brownfield sites may be the only natural greenspace there is. They are our unofficial countryside: an escape from the noise, bustle and pollution of London and, if properly managed, they could help significantly to reduce the number of areas deficient in accessible open space.

Clearly, not all urban wasteland sites meet these needs. Some are perceived to be unsafe, unappealing and the focus for anti-social activity. In some cases in London, the value of wastelands has been recognised and they are being actively managed as wildlife sites for the benefit of local communities. Other wastelands are more likely to be inaccessible to the public and targeted for development. Their potential to fulfil a much-needed function for people and wildlife is unrecognised or ignored by both planners and developers.

Contamination and creative remediation

Many brownfield sites remain contaminated as a result of their previous industrial use and are a threat to public health and safety. Yet it is often these abandoned sites, with their unusual substrates, that host distinctive plants.

We realise that remediation work required to make contaminated sites safe is a costly and complex obstacle to redevelopment. We agree that health and safety issues must be tackled. But the impact of remediation and redevelopment on wildlife must also be considered early on. Mitigation, in the form of innovative wasteland habitat creation, may be one option for compensating loss of existing biodiversity.

At a former Transco site in Deptford, L.B. Lewisham, contaminated ground has being tackled in preparation for a new education and visitor centre. The top half-metre of contaminated substrate has been removed and replaced with crushed brick and concrete as remediation to allow the local flora and fauna to recolonise naturally.

Undervalued and ignored

The wildlife value of brownfield land is often unrecognised, despite the biodiversity of even the smallest sites.

London is fortunate to have a relatively good history of habitat surveying across the boroughs. Small wasteland sites, however, have in the past, been under-sampled because they fell below the size threshold of accepted survey methodology. The biodiversity of newly abandoned wasteland can also develop quickly but its value may not be acknowledged if a habitat survey is not due for several years.

Ecological research and the evaluation of wasteland habitat has lagged behind that of more conventional semi-natural habitats of the British countryside. As a result, nature conservation professionals consistently undervalue wasteland sites.

As we have explained, the Government has set targets for building homes on brownfield or previously-developed land. These are contained in *Planning Policy Guidance Note 3 (Housing)*, which defines what is meant by 'previously-developed'. This definition specifically excludes the following: 'land that was previously developed but where remains of any structure or activity have blended into the landscape in the process of time (to the extent that it can reasonably be considered as part of the natural surroundings), and where there is a clear reason that could outweigh the re-use of the site – such as its contribution to nature conservation'.

This exclusion clause has offered a 'safety net' to a few mature brownfield sites and has led to a more sensitive approach to redevelopment. However, most urban wastelands are at earlier stages of colonisation and do not meet the conventional idea of 'blending in'. These wastelands tend to be viewed instead as unsightly wildlife deserts, when in fact they can be of the highest wildlife value. London Wildlife Trust believes that if this value were recognised by environmental professionals these sites could be saved or mitigation made for their loss.

Notes

1 London's wildlife sites have been surveyed and assessed using procedures recommended by the London Ecology Unit, and now adopted by the London Mayor and the Greater London Authority's Strategy Directorate.

2 Sites of Metropolitan Importance are sites which contain the best examples of London's habitats, sites which contain particularly rare species, rare assemblages of species or important populations of species. They are of the highest priority for protection.

■ The above is an extract from a report by London Wildlife Trust on behalf of the London Brownfields Forum. For more information visit their web site which can be found at www.wildlondon.org.uk or see their address details on page 41.

© London Wildlife Trust

500,000 new homes for M11 region

Eastern counties reeling as assembly approves huge housing expansion from the Wash to the Thames

Plans to build half a million homes between the Wash and the Thames by 2021 were approved 5 February 2004 by the eastern regional assembly despite Essex and Hertfordshire councils' belief that the counties could not cope with the additions.

The main area for growth would be the M11 corridor between north London, Stansted and Cambridge, much of it on green belt.

The decision was made under pressure from the planning minister, Lord Rooker, who insisted that the area between London and Cambridge was 'a growth corridor'.

This area was at first either side of the M11 but has been widened and extended north to provide more space for housing. It now includes Peterborough, the whole of Cambridgeshire, parts of north Hertfordshire, including Stevenage, and other areas in Essex.

Yesterday at a meeting in Hertford 478,000 of the new properties were 'distributed' among the eastern counties and the assembly agreed to find land for another 18,000.

Hertfordshire, where most of the undeveloped land is green belt, had agreed to try to find space for 50,000 homes but the county was allocated 72,000 and fears it will get a large share of the additional 18,000 as well. A spokesman said at least 25,000 would have to go on greenfield sites. Essex has been told it must find room for 131,000 homes.

With the government backing expansion at Stansted and Luton airports the eastern counties nearest London were said at the meeting 'to feel as if they are inside a pressure cooker coming to the boil'.

In Hertfordshire alone the housing allocation means building

By Paul Brown,
Environment Correspondent

two new towns, one the size of St Albans and another comparable to Stevenage, in the next 20 years. Harlow, in Essex, would have to expand dramatically.

> *The main area for growth would be the M11 corridor between north London, Stansted and Cambridge, much of it on green belt*

Derrick Ashley, a Hertfordshire county councillor, said that the government was turning south-east England into a kind of Hong Kong, an industrial and commercial powerhouse for the UK. 'This may be good for economic growth but it is not in the best social and environmental interests of the country as a whole. What is needed in the south-east is

social housing but this kind of numbers game does not address this issue at all.'

He said Hertfordshire was already the most overcrowded county in England. 'What concerns, apart from losing our greenfields, is that the roads, rail links, hospitals and schools are already overstretched yet there are no plans for the government to address these issues. How are the extra people going to get about on the M25, M11, M1 and on the railway lines that are already overcrowded?'

A Hertfordshire and Essex joint proposal that was put before the eastern regional assembly meeting in Hertford yesterday to reduce the number of new homes to 442,000, was rejected.

Hertfordshire council said in a statement that a shadow had fallen over the county.

Mr Ashley said: 'Decisions about the future of Hertfordshire are being made by an unelected body that does not properly represent the people of Hertfordshire.' He said powers for strategic planning had been taken away from the county councils and given to a regional body which was pushing them through at the behest of the government.

He added: 'The assembly has rushed into making decisions without a proper assessment of the true environmental impact and infrastructure requirements, not to mention the added pressure that the expansion of Stansted and Luton airports will have on our already overburdened road and rail network.'

There will be a period of public consultation over the decision prior to a public inquiry in the summer of 2005. The government is then expected to approve the plan during 2006.

Building problems for the future

Giving public money to private developers may speed affordable housebuilding. But developers' main focus is profit not building communities where people want to live

By James Tickell

In the next housing bill the government has now confirmed that it plans to give public funds for private developers to build affordable housing. Until now, this funding has only been available to not-for-profit housing associations, which are intensively regulated by the government's housing agency, the Housing Corporation.

Why is the government taking this step? The private sector has not universally distinguished itself in its use of public money in other sectors – the railways spring to mind. Problems with over-complex private finance initiative (PFI) schemes for schools and hospitals are common.

So there must surely be strong evidence that the special skills of private developers are desperately needed to help government deliver on its building plans? Well, no. The evidence in favour of this new measure is minimal.

Predictably we learn that some private developers think it would be a good idea. No surprises there. But are housing associations inefficient developers? After all, they've been competing for government grants for decades, and if anything have a reputation for over-competitiveness. There's certainly no firm evidence that private developers, faced with the same intensive regulatory framework, would be any more efficient. If anything, housing associations should have an edge: they can access private funding at far lower rates than developers, and don't need to pay profits to shareholders.

More importantly though, there is plenty of evidence that housing associations take a considered and community-focused approach to new developments. They are in the business of creating places where people want to live, and have long-term commitments to the areas where they work. Any surpluses they generate are reinvested into more housing and local services.

> **If private developers are to take the lead on developments, clearly their priority has to be the creation of shareholder value**

When affordable housing is a part of a wider scheme, associations act as the community advocates. Their job is to ensure that affordable housing is not fenced off at the edge of a new development, but integrated into the wider community. Associations invest much time and effort into partnership working with local authorities. This is all integral to their social purpose: to be in business for neighbourhoods.

If private developers are to take the lead on developments, clearly their priority has to be the creation of shareholder value. Long-term community building simply is not what they do.

It will be said that associations should have little to fear from competition, if they are so efficient. But will the competition be fair? Developers will not face the cost of dealing with long-term government regulation. They will be able to cherry-pick the major and more lucrative projects, extract the profits, and move on. They will have no interest in providing the rented homes that are vitally needed for a flexible and mobile workforce.

The major risk in this ill-considered proposal is that it will marginalise and underfund the real work of community building, leaving affordable housing as mass-produced 'boxes' built to low standards, and the occupants without access to the support and services they need.

■ James Tickell is Deputy Chief Executive of the National Housing Federation .

© Guardian Newspapers Limited 2004

Wanted: new city to solve UK housing crisis

By Kamal Ahmed and
Jamie Doward

Britain will need a new city the size of Leeds to be built over the next decade if it is to tackle the chronic housing shortage which leads to rocketing house prices that keep potential first-time buyers off the property ladder.

In a consultation document passed to the government-funded review of the state of Britain's housing supply, the House Builders' Federation (HBF) says that 55,000 more houses a year need to be built to keep up with demand. Over 20 years that would mean more than half a million additional new homes.

The study by the HBF, which represents construction companies that build 80 per cent of homes in England and Wales, says archaic planning laws coupled with what one official described as a virulent 'anti-housing lobby' meant that too many new developments were being blocked.

Planning inquiries can take years and the Government's demand for more inexpensive social housing means that many sites are no longer worth developing commercially, the HBF said.

The crisis is affecting the poorest parts of the country. The number of households in England which have been classed as homeless this year is set to top 200,000 for the first time in a decade.

The figure highlights an acute shortage of affordable housing, pricing families out of the market amid accusations that the Government has repeatedly failed to tackle homelessness.

The findings come four days before the Government publishes the Treasury review into the housing market by Bank of England official Kate Barker. She will say that planning laws need to be streamlined and that 'nimbyism' – the 'not in my back yard' attitude of many communities – must be tackled.

She will admit there is a widespread shortage of housing that is affecting economic growth and the ability of families to live where they choose.

The number of households in England which have been classed as homeless this year is set to top 200,000 for the first time in a decade

Public service workers are also often priced out of the market in city areas, particularly the South East and London, and have to live a long way from their work.

'To meet the need created simply by the growth in the number of households, housebuilding in England needs to expand by approximately 55,000 dwellings a year to around 190,000 a year, or 215,000 new homes a year in Britain,' the HBF report says.

'It is clear that annual housing supply is well below the levels required. As well as the obvious social consequences of long-term housing under-provision, the damaging economic consequences are now fully appreciated by the Treasury.

'The housing affordability crisis in southern England, a consequence of under-supply over two decades, is having an impact on areas such as health, education and transport, which face serious difficulties recruiting key workers who are unable to afford the high cost of housing.'

■ This article first appeared in *The Observer*, 7 December 2003.
© *Guardian Newspapers Limited 2004*

Household growth in England

Average annual increase in households

	Projected 1996-2001 000 p.a.	Actual 1996-2001 000 p.a.
North East	3.8	3.5
North West	12.6	15.5
Yorkshire and Humber	12.0	11.3
East Midlands	15.2	15.3
West Midlands	12.2	12.5
East of England	23.6	29.5
Greater London	25.2	46.0
South East	35.6	39.3
South West	21.2	23.5
England	161.2	196.5

Source: DETR, 1999; DTLR, 2001

Have I got the house for you

John Prescott's big idea is to get key workers to move out of London and into one of the new homes being built outside the capital. But will people be prepared to move?

By Mary O'Hara

Will London's hard-pressed public sector workers swap their cramped inner-city flats for shiny new houses surrounded by green fields and a view across the mouth of the Thames? The deputy prime minister, John Prescott, thinks so and is prepared to spend billions of pounds backing his big idea.

But an investigation by *Jobs & Money* paints a different picture of Britain's so-called housing revolution. The houses, often looking like a collection of boxes stapled together next to a patch of garden, are more likely to be built on the contaminated remains of old gasworks than farmland – and the view across the river can be disturbed by a landscape of factories and other industrial delights.

That might fit the environmental brief which says we must only build on brownfield sights, but has led to fears on the grounds that the new estates will go the same way as many of the post-war new towns, like Bracknell, which has a central shopping area so bleak that bulldozers are due to flatten it.

Local people are fearful that an influx of single people and young families from London will push up property prices and, without adequate amenities, bring the kind of social problems that beset many parts of the capital itself.

Mr Prescott announced last month the final phase of his 'communities' plan for easing the housing shortage in the south-east of England – the construction of 300,000 homes. They are to be built by 2016 across the south-east; 120,000 of them will be along the Thames Gateway, east of London. This is on top of the estimated 1.1m homes that planners had already accounted for across the region over the same period.

The first stage of development – from now until 2006 – is expected to cost £2bn and will reach as far as Corby in the south Midlands. It is being billed as the largest house-building programme since the new towns sprang up 50 years ago.

> *The first stage of development – from now until 2006 – is expected to cost £2bn and will reach as far as Corby in the south Midlands*

The most recently confirmed initiative, Thames Gateway, will stretch along the river from Stratford in the east of the capital out across southern Essex and north Kent, and is to be built on a mixture of brownfield land and greenfield sites. *Jobs & Money* went to Rochester – one of the government's 'strategic' areas in the Thames Gateway – to visit Rochester Riverside, a 30-hectare site bordering the River Medway earmarked for some of the central government funds. We wanted to see at first hand what sort of site the government's plans are based on and what the real potential is.

Riverside is just a few minutes' walk from the historic old town across a busy dual carriageway. Today it is waste ground, strewn with debris, overgrown weeds and interspersed with the occasional builders' merchants. The main London railway line runs along one side of the site, meaning that access is limited to a few narrow arches.

The site is also the location of two imposing, 50ft-high circular gas distributors – which alone constitute a huge, three-year decontamination problem before any building can commence. Despite being for the most part derelict, Riverside has been of interest to private developers for years, but they have all abandoned any plans for cost reasons.

Decontaminating brownfield sites is one of the primary reasons so many have remained untouched for so long, but the government now believes that by harnessing public and private funds, sites like Riverside can be transformed. Some 2,000 new homes could be on the site by 2016 if the complex planning requirements can be met. Owned by Medway Council and managed with the South East of England Development Agency (Seeda), Riverside's derelict state is typical of many of the brownfield sites targeted for the new cash.

It placates the environmental lobby by not being green fields, it can be converted wholesale, and it is within a reasonable distance of transport links. There is also the important factor of affordability. A sizeable slice (around 25%) of the properties could be designated as affordable housing for key workers.

However, it is also typical of the problems the government faces in pushing its initiatives through. Firstly, conversion of contaminated brownfield sites is neither easy nor quick and it will therefore have no immediate impact on housing shortages.

Secondly, there is a real concern that people will refuse to live on land that was once contaminated, and even though the Riverside site is next to the river, the view is of an industrial estate. The site is also at risk of flooding and requires significant protection measures.

Thirdly, 2,000 properties will make only a slight dent in the local housing shortage, never mind an over-spill from the capital. 'Affordable housing is all well and good,' Martha Hamilton, one resident, told us, 'but there are already lots of younger people here who are desperate to get on the ladder and can't afford it. They need more homes to be built.'

According to Halifax's latest figures, the average price of a property in Rochester stands at £154,027 compared with the national average of £132,000. The local residents we spoke to say they are concerned that prices are already so high that even with a proportion of properties listed as 'affordable', the question is: affordable for whom?

This brings us to the government's aim of generating an influx of key workers from London to the Thames Gateway, who would then commute to work. Residents appear concerned that this only makes the problems of access and affordability for local people worse.

'It's a good idea to build more houses,' Ms Hamilton says, 'but it has to benefit the local community.'

Another Rochester resident says: 'They also need to be thinking about schools and other facilities like

What Prescott is planning

Where the 300,000 new homes are to be built by 2016

Thames Gateway
Some 120,000 new homes are planned, primarily to be built on brownfield sites. The area has the largest (3,000 acres) collection of brownfield sites close to a European capital.

Five priority areas have been identified: Stratford and Lower Lea which are to get 15,000 new homes, Barking and Dagenham which will get the same, North Kent Thameside with 25,000, Greenwich, Woolwich and Thamesmead with 20,000, Medway Riverside in Kent with 10,000 and Thurrock with 5,000. A further 30,000 homes will be spread across other gateway areas.

South Midlands
The areas most likely to benefit from the expansion plans are Corby, Kettering and Wellingborough which between them will see about 33,000 new homes built.

Northampton and Milton Keynes
These will be among the biggest beneficiaries. Milton Keynes is to be significantly expanded with a 32,600 boost to housing while Northampton's tally of homes is set to grow by 22,000.

Bedford, Luton and Aylesbury Vale
Part of the western flank of the housing expansion, Bedford and Luton will get 29,400 new homes between them on the fringes of the towns and beyond into greenfield sites, while Aylesbury Vale is in line for 16,400.

Harlow
The plans are at the very early stages and subject to further study, the government says, but an estimated 26,400 new properties are likely to be built.

Ashford
10,000 new homes on some brownfield sites but environmental lobbyists believe it may impinge on more green belt than is currently claimed.
Total number of homes: approx 300,000 subject to plans. Cost: Phase one: 2003-2006 – £2bn (includes initial cost of clearing and decontamination of brownfield sites).

Other plans
At Stansted and Cambridge a further 190,000 homes could be planned along the M11 corridor subject to feasibility studies.

Source: Office of the Deputy Prime Minister

that. This is an already heavily populated area.'

Andy Elliot, of the Halifax estate agency covering Chatham and Gillingham, says recent price surges in the area have made it much harder for local key workers to get on the property ladder. Even more people coming in from London would make the problem of affordability 'worse and worse', he says. 'We have already been getting people coming from London because the area has been cheap,' he says. 'But the government really has to make sure that it looks at the issue of affordability closely. There is always going to be a problem with shortages of property – but if there is going to be more of an overflow from London, this will affect prices.'

With all of these concerns in mind we also visited one brownfield site in the full throes of development – St Mary's Island in Chatham. St Mary's is an island connected to the rest of Chatham by a road bridge. It took three years to decontaminate, according to Seeda, and about one-third of the island's housing quota (around 800 properties) is finished. It has taken seven years so far with five or six years still to go.

The houses are a mixture of basic Barratt 'box' properties and flats and some more imaginative designs painted in bright pastels, boasting expansive windows and balconies. Some even have solar panels.

A third of the land is designated for green space, and work is about to begin on a doctors' surgery and community centre. The island is about 10 minutes' walk from Chatham's flagship commercial development, Chatham Maritime, with its shops and marina. With one bus and a train, commuters can be in London in about an hour and a half.

So what's the catch? Well, an hour-and-a-half commute each way every day is not very tempting. And there's the prospect of living in a self-contained residential area, cut off from the centre of civic life. A community that has not developed organically may not appeal to everyone.

The properties are also high density, to meet government aims of getting more homes per square foot.

Pros and Cons

For:
- A proportion of the homes being built will be set aside as 'affordable' and targeted at key workers in the capital.
- Most areas have reasonable transport links or increased investment in them.
- Developers must work within government guidelines: a range of property types, green spaces and amenities.
- There are good schools near some sites, but new ones may be needed.

Against:
- It could be more than a decade before anyone can move in.
- The projects are essentially experiments and workers cannot be compelled to move out of London.
- Sites will be decontaminated, but may still be of concern to some people.
- Increases in supply may not result in an easing of house price inflation.
- Local facilities may be over-stretched.

And, even if a house has a riverside view, it is of a power station. Oh, and there's also the pesky prospect of the airport that might be built a few hundred yards away on the other side of the river.

And let's not forget that all-important factor: price. According to Seeda, which oversees the scheme along with Medway council and developers, Countryside Property, prices range from £150,000 to £350,000. In other words, they start

at around £15,000 more than the price of the average Chatham property – £134,000, according to Halifax. So, while around a quarter will be designated for affordable housing, a teacher on a salary of £25,000 a year in Chatham – never mind in London with the added cost of commuting – can forget about it.

Andy Elliot of Halifax says: 'St Mary's Island is an example of good properties being built but we struggle to sell the flats because people know they can get something much cheaper a mile up the road. Some of the flats on St Mary's end up being bought as second homes.'

But there's something else too. So far, most of the people who have moved to the island are local – multiple branches of whole families, in some instances. Seeda is about to do a survey to see who the second wave of residents are likely to be – but if they are not key workers from London, the government may need to get its thinking cap on.

As soon as the deputy prime minister, who has responsibility for housing and regeneration, triumphantly announced his plans, the cavalcade of criticism and warnings flooded in. Environmentalists such as the Campaign to Protect Rural England warned that the amount of greenfield sites earmarked was higher than it should be. Builders' organisations cautioned that there might not be enough skilled construction workers to meet the targets. And sceptics of all hues, including opposition politicians, said not enough thought had been put into transport and infrastructure.

John Prescott's speech was big on numbers and low on substance. Many of the plans are just that – plans – and there are worries that they are not drastic enough, ambitious enough, or coming quickly enough.

The government is staring at an estimated population growth of 2m people per decade, much of which will be in the south-east. The number of first-time buyers is at an all-time low and they are finding it harder to raise deposits.

There is also the problem of social change. The growth in family breakdown and later marriages means more single occupation households, resulting in an ever-upwards curve of demand for property. All this at a time when the average number of new homes being built is at an all-time low, according to the government's own figures.

These are all issues John Prescott says he thinks that the latest initiatives will help to address. 'The money I am allocating will help to kickstart the process of turning Europe's largest collection of brownfield sites into communities where people are proud to belong,' he said.

The deputy PM also said that £600m had been set aside for transport projects across the Gateway in an effort to confront the reality that more people mean more traffic and greater pressure on public transport. Some of the key strategic areas, such as Ebbsfleet in north Kent, are deliberately on the route of the new Channel Tunnel Rail Link.

'Today marks the start of a long-term commitment coupled with a long-term process of delivery,' Mr Prescott said. But this, critics argue, is precisely the problem. Many of the

plans will take years to come to fruition. It is not even certain if the money available will be enough or if the 2016 deadline is realistic.

Perhaps less certain is whether any government, no matter how much cash it injects, can successfully socially engineer the sort of communities people want to live in. Londoners cannot be forced to move to Medway any more than they can be forced to move to Manchester. Watch this space.

120,000 new homes on the way

By Charles Clover, Environment Editor

John Prescott, the Deputy Prime Minister, yesterday identified growth areas where at least 120,000 homes will be built along the Thames by 2016 to ease the housing shortage in the South-East.

The five areas – east London, Greenwich and Woolwich, Barking Reach, Thurrock and North Kent-Thameside – are at the heart of Government ambitions to build 200,000 houses more than currently planned in the region.

Mr Prescott said £330 million would be spent in those areas over the next three years on 100 projects to open up key development sites.

He also divided money he announced last year between three other growth areas, Milton Keynes, London-Stansted and Cambridge, and Ashford in Kent.

Urban development corporations – described by developers as 'mini Canary Wharfs' – are to be set up in the Thurrock and London parts of the Thames Gateway, as the East London-Essex-North Kent corridor is known, and in Northampton, to drive things through at local level. Weaker 'partnership' arrangements will prevail elsewhere in Essex and North Kent.

Mr Prescott said the £330 million in Government spending on infrastructure and £600 million on

improving transport links would bring in at least £1 billion to £2 billion from other public and private partners.

But the scale of the task he has set himself was underlined by the admission in his own document that the plans would provide only 40,000 homes above current targets in the Thames Gateway.

> 'We see economic logic in concentrating growth around high-speed transport corridors such as the Channel Tunnel Rail Link'

The Government also announced a joint English Partnerships/ Housing Corporation competition to develop 56 sites in former new towns, producing up to 1,300 housing association homes by 2005.

Mr Prescott said: 'The money I am allocating will help to kick-start

the process of turning Europe's largest collection of brownfield sites into communities where people are proud to belong.'

The announcement, however, alarmed conservationists because the Thurrock development corporation will be given sway over Thurrock's green belt, raising fears that developers might regenerate brownfield sites in return for greenfield land.

Ebbsfleet in north Kent, a major station on the Channel Tunnel Rail Link to be completed in 2007, has been identified as a commercial area where some of the 180,000 jobs the Government is promising along the Thames Gateway will be found.

There will also be new housing between Dartford and Gravesend. Stratford, three miles east of the City and already a major train intersection and another link on the new Channel Tunnel route, is seen as the centre-piece of the bid for the 2012 Olympics.

Mr Prescott said: 'We see economic logic in concentrating growth around high-speed transport corridors such as the Channel Tunnel Rail Link.'

David Davis, the shadow deputy prime minister, said that the green belt should not be sacrificed to create 'high-stress dormitory towns'.

Urban land in Britain

Meeting the targets

The need to conserve our wildlife sites and forests, and the need to use our agricultural land means that we need to limit as much as possible the spread of urban areas into the countryside. However there are still many demands on greenfield land – from out-of-town developments to roads and houses. Indeed, before 2016 it is predicted that England alone will have to accommodate an additional 4.4 million households.

Current business-as-usual housing practices will take over 80,000 hectares of greenfield sites by 2016. This is an area larger than Exmoor.

Meeting the targets: homes in cities

We argue though that this demand can be met almost entirely within existing towns and cities. The desire for this is not just to do with protecting the countryside. A large proportion of the increase in road traffic has come about due to suburban sprawl and inner-city decay. Today, people's homes are much further away from their work, from shops, libraries, cinemas, friends. Reinvesting in cities can cut the need to travel, and increase people's quality of life all round.

Sunderland
Sunderland's Development Plan recognises the need for increasing densities in cities. It states that 'There are also benefits to be gained from locating higher density housing closer to shops and community facilities as this also minimises the need to travel by car ... in urban terms higher densities enable a return to the traditional street rather than suburban type estates.'

All of the 4.4 million dwellings needed in England, plus equivalent numbers for Scotland, Northern Ireland and Wales could be provided in cities.

Friends of the Earth

1) Empty properties
There are 997,000 empty homes in the UK, 4.1% of the stock. Government-owned stock is 16% vacant. 6% of properties in London are empty. Meeting the Royal Commission on Environmental Pollution's target would add 516,000 properties to the housing stock.

Best London authorities
If each London borough achieved Harrow's vacancy rate for the private sector, Barnet's for local authority housing, and Sutton's for Housing Association property, there would be 103,000 fewer empty properties in London.

2) Increasing densities in housing
As the housing stock is redeveloped, increased densities could provide for 2 million households. There are barriers to overcome here – currently development plans require that too much land is given over to cars for example, and there is a perception that increasing densities means town-cramming. There are limits to intensification, as the failed experiments of 1960s tower-block living have shown, but our suggested density levels – 260 people per hectare – do not approach them.

3) Use of derelict sites, conversion of commercial space above shops, and conversion of large houses to flats
These measures could easily provide homes for over 2 million households. Again, there are obstacles here. Currently VAT is charged on refurbishment and redevelopment, but not on new-build – one of the factors leading the Living Over The Shop campaign to say 'despite the widespread concern about the need to repopulate town centres, the level of conversion work is lower than in 1992'. Indeed, redevelopment overall is taking place so slowly that it will take 4,000 years at current rates to replace the housing stock.

■ The above information is from Friends of the Earth's web site which can be found at www.foe.co.uk
© Friends of the Earth

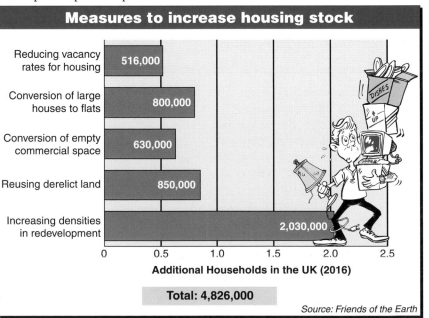

Measures to increase housing stock

Measure	Additional Households in the UK (2016)
Reducing vacancy rates for housing	516,000
Conversion of large houses to flats	800,000
Conversion of empty commercial space	630,000
Reusing derelict land	850,000
Increasing densities in redevelopment	2,030,000

Total: 4,826,000

Source: Friends of the Earth

Communities not concrete

Information from the Campaign to Protect Rural England

Introduction

The Government published its Sustainable Communities Plan in February 2003. This document, and nine accompanying ones which cover each English region, set out the Government's latest housing policies over the next 15-30 years in both urban and rural areas. The plan has important implications for the countryside.

What is the problem?

Vast areas of countryside and small communities are under threat from Government housing plans.

The Government's Sustainable Communities Plan proposes massive development to meet a growing need for housing. Four large zones in the South Midlands, South East and East of England have been earmarked for particularly intensive growth: Milton Keynes/South Midlands, London-Stansted-Cambridge ('the M11 corridor'), the Thames Gateway and Ashford in Kent.

Government studies indicate that up to half a million homes could be built on greenfield land in these growth areas over the next 30 years. This number of new houses would, in itself, cover an area of some 44 square miles – the size of Newcastle upon Tyne. And further countryside will be consumed to provide the roads, workplaces and shops associated with all those new houses and cars.

A threat to urban renewal

Over recent years we have supported the Government's development of improved policies on planning for new housing and urban renewal. Its Sustainable Communities Plan carries some of these policies forward, but also poses serious threats. The major greenfield development proposals implied by the plan could be at great expense to the environment and declining urban areas both elsewhere in the region and across the country. CPRE is worried about

Campaign to Protect Rural England

the plan's potential impact on the pursuit of more balanced regional development. Much depends on how the programme of action set out in the plan is implemented on the ground. Lack of local public transport means that more housing could result in more car-based commuting and more road congestion.

A top-down approach

We welcome the Government's emphasis on better use of land, improved design and affordable housing. However, we are deeply

---

Vast areas of countryside and small communities are under threat from Government housing plans

---

concerned about its top-down centralising approach, which could undermine public involvement and accountability in planning.

What is the solution?

We would like to see the Government apply five sustainability tests to its proposals for development:

1. Environmental capacity

New housebuilding should be tested regionally and locally against environmental capacity constraints, rather than imposed as targets from the top down.

2. Better use of resources

Development must make much better use of land and other natural resources, such as energy and minerals. Sprawling housing estates disconnected from jobs and services that waste land and generate traffic should not be allowed.

3. Redevelopment of brownfield sites

There should be higher targets for the re-use of brownfield sites, previously developed urban land and buildings.

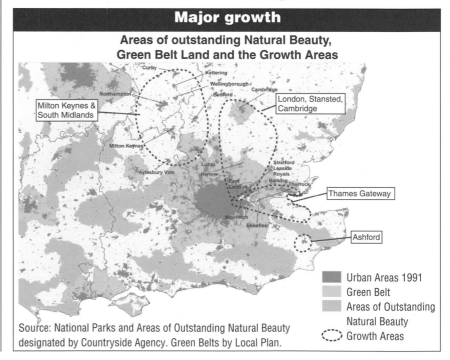

Major growth

Areas of outstanding Natural Beauty, Green Belt Land and the Growth Areas

Milton Keynes & South Midlands

London, Stansted, Cambridge

Thames Gateway

Ashford

Urban Areas 1991
Green Belt
Areas of Outstanding Natural Beauty
Growth Areas

Source: National Parks and Areas of Outstanding Natural Beauty designated by Countryside Agency. Green Belts by Local Plan.

4. Even regions

There should be a coherent Government strategy to share prosperity across all regions in England and reduce regional disparities.

5. Public involvement

There should be genuine opportunities for the public to have a say in decisions on new development in their area.

What CPRE is doing

Through our national Communities not Concrete campaign, we are calling for the Government's proposals to be delivered in the most sustainable way for communities across the whole country.

We would like to see development that:
■ protects the countryside
■ assists urban renewal
■ improves everyone's quality of life

We have commissioned an environmental critique that is looking at how the Government proposals could be delivered better. We are also producing newsletters and leaflets to let the public know about the implications of the proposals, and why we're so concerned about them and to encourage people to take up the chance to comment on them.

Across the country, we are actively engaged in looking at these

proposals and assessing how different counties or regions could be affected by them.

We have responded formally to three of the plans. CPRE Kent has responded to the draft Ashford strategy and we have responded nationally to the M11 Corridor study and the Milton Keynes and South Midlands sub-regional strategy.

What you can do

Help publicise the implications of the strategy

Our branches need help in alerting the public to the implications of these development plans. If you can organise a public meeting, write press releases or distribute leaflets, please contact them.

Write to your MP

Write to your local MP asking him or her to encourage the Government to apply the five sustainability tests to their housing and development proposals.

Join our letter-writing team

We could really use your written help with some of our campaigns. Our letter-writing team of members and supporters writes letters from time to time to key 'opinion formers' like local MPs, a Government department or a member of the House of Lords. Won't you join us? The letters we ask people to write are straightforward, politically balanced and don't take long to write. We supply suggested text highlighting key points, which you are free to amend. We would ask you to write a couple of letters a year.

Join CPRE

Join CPRE and become a member of a dynamic network of 59,000 other people all working to promote and protect our countryside.

■ The Campaign to Protect Rural England (CPRE) exists to promote the beauty, tranquillity and diversity of rural England by encouraging the sustainable use of land and other natural resources in town and country. For further information on their work and campaigns, visit their web site which can be found at www.cpre.org.uk Alternatively, see page 41 for their address details.

© The Campaign to Protect Rural England (CPRE)

The rural housing crisis

Information from the Country Land and Business Association

Government policy threatens to exacerbate the growing housing crisis in the countryside,' warns Mark Hudson, President of the Country Land and Business Association which today publishes its report, *Housing the Rural Economy*.

'The basic needs of rural communities for local housing have been forgotten in the Government's top-down approach to housing demand. Local authorities are struggling to reach affordable rural housing targets whilst large-scale developments on the edges of towns

Country Land & Business Association
RURAL ECONOMY IS OUR BUSINESS

are allowed to take precedence over small, sympathetic housing schemes that allow villages to grow naturally.

'Now the Government is proposing to do away with key planning guidelines and that will only worsen the rural housing crisis, increasing the gap between demand and supply and threatening the economic base of our villages.'

The CLA's report, *Housing the Rural Economy*, proposes a series of practical solutions to open up more land and opportunities for rural housing. It also accuses the Government of neglecting the needs of 13 million people who live and work in the countryside and face increasingly inadequate housing provision along with escalating house prices which far exceed their earnings.

'House prices now lie out of the reach of much of the rural-based population,' continues Mark Hudson. 'Unless the housing situation improves, people will continue to drift or be forced to move away. Local jobs will be put at risk along with local services and facilities. In short, the rural economy will suffer.'

The report calls for policy changes on several fronts. The Government's withdrawal of Local Authority Special Housing Grant has left a large hole in funding for affordable housing which will more than cancel out the increase in the Housing Corporation's Approved Development Programme planned over the next two years.

At the same time, the proposed withdrawal of the exception site policy, which allows affordable housing to be built on sites that would not normally be granted planning permission, will restrict appropriate, small-scale housing schemes.

'House prices now lie out of the reach of much of the rural-based population . . . unless the housing situation improves, people will continue to drift or be forced to move away'

The report also challenges the current stranglehold on the use of redundant farm buildings for housing

– another example of where Government policy fails to make use of existing resources to meet housing demand.

The report makes 17 recommendations to boost rural housing in England and Wales, including:
- a requirement for planning authorities to meet local housing need close to its origin through the organic growth of villages, with more allowance for housing to be built on the edge of existing villages
- more weight given to the use of redundant farm buildings for housing, along with a change in the definition of 'brownfield sites' to include land previously used for agriculture, which would free up more land for housing
- the retention of the exception site policy, with the further possibility of developers being

allowed to 'cross-subsidise' affordable housing schemes through the construction and sale of open-market houses
- guidelines on housing provision in settlements of fewer than 3,000 people in greenbelts, national parks and areas of outstanding beauty to mirror the rest of the countryside
- the revenue raised from additional council tax on second homes to be used by local authorities to support affordable housing in rural areas
- the implementation of Government proposals to allow houses to be built for locally-based workers in rural businesses

'Rural communities and businesses are not calling for a revolution in housing,' adds Mark Hudson. 'But they do insist that policies at national, regional and local level must help, not hinder, the provision of rural housing, and that a concerted effort is now made to tackle the growing crisis.

'Our recommendations are not a charter for concreting the country-side. Rather, they are practical proposals to Government, local councils and planners, housing associations and landowners to sustain rural communities and help them to thrive. Part of our job will be to support some of the more imaginative rural housing solutions being pioneered in different parts of the country.'

Housing the Rural Economy was produced by a working group of CLA members in consultation with professional planners, housing associations and others active in the provision of rural housing.

Exception site guidelines enable local planning authorities to grant permission for affordable housing for small sites, within and around existing villages, which under the local plan would not otherwise be released for housing.

- The above information is from the Country Land and Business Association's (CLA) web site: www.cla.org.uk Alternatively see their address details on page 41.

...CAN'T SEE ANY YOUNG PEOPLE...

-CAN YOU SEE ANY NEW HOUSES?

The unaffordable cost of affordable housing

Britain's housing crisis is being made worse by the policies introduced to solve it

For the first time, evidence shows that some local councils are increasing demands on developers for affordable housing in the knowledge that this will, in practice, further constrain new housing development

This results in ideal sites being left abandoned, reducing the supply of both open market and social housing which are necessary to help overcome Britain's rapidly worsening shortage of housing.

With undersupply being the root cause of house price inflation, current planning policy is set to exacerbate the shortage putting even more long-term upward pressure on prices and worsening the housing prospects for first-time buyers, key workers and all those on low or moderate incomes.

The House Builders' Federation believes this situation stems from either a lack of understanding of basic economic principles or the deliberate misuse of central government policy by local planning authorities.

Pierre Williams, spokesman for the House Builders' Federation, said: 'Everyone wants more "affordable" housing but few are willing to acknowledge that this affordability comes at a price to both taxpayer and developer.

'Affordable housing is, in reality, subsidised housing. It is who pays this subsidy that counts. With far too little public money available for a major house-building programme, local authorities are increasing their demands for private developers to build it for them as a condition of providing planning permission. These demands have reached a level where developers can no longer afford to build.

'This catch-22 situation arises from the reluctance to accept that private developers cannot, and will

not, take on loss-making projects. But evidence is also emerging that some local councils are demanding more affordable housing – not to help first-time buyers – but in the knowledge that they can stop development whilst maintaining political correctness.

'This exploits the divergence of central Government housing policy. We know the shortage of homes pushes up prices. And we know the taxpayer cannot afford to pay for all the so-called 'affordable' homes. So what we really need is a planning system that lets private developers fix this problem.'

Housing in Britain
Population, households and dwellings
- The UK population grew by 0.25% per year (145,700 p.a.) from 1981 to 1991 and 0.37% per year (215,800 p.a.) from 1991 to 2000. Net international migration accounted for 62% of UK population growth between 1995-6 and 1999-2000.
- The number of households in Great Britain grew by 1.0% per year from 1981 to 1991 (220,000 p.a.) and 0.9% per year (220,400 p.a.) from 1991 to 2000. Average annual increases in the number of households in England during the 1990s were the second largest of any decade (after the 1970s) since records begin in the mid 19th century.
- In 1981 there were approximately 4% more dwellings than house-

holds in England, just sufficient to provide a home for every household and leave a margin for vacant dwellings. But in the last 20 years household growth has far exceeded expansion of the housing stock, so that this surplus had fallen to 0.2% by 2000. Yet 3.6% of dwellings in England were vacant in April 2000 and 7.6% were classified as unfit in 1996.
- With the exception of London in the 1980s, household growth exceeded housing stock expansion in all of the English regions from 1981 to 1991 and 1991 to 2000. By 2000, there were 4.2% fewer homes in London than house-holds, with 1.4% fewer homes than households in the South East.
- Analysis of trends since the 1930s indicates that, over the longer term, household growth is largely independent of growth in the housing stock.

Land and people
- The proportion of Britain's population living in urban areas (90%) is the second highest in Europe and the sixth highest in the world (excluding several city and small island states).
- To accommodate expected household growth, it has been estimated that the urban area of England will increase from 10.6% in 1991 to 11.9% by 2016. So urban expansion takes 0.05% of England's land area each year, or 1% every 20 years. Typically housing accounts for about seven-tenths of land in urban uses.
- 16% of England's land area is designated as Areas of Outstanding Natural Beauty (20,393 sq km), 12% as Green Belt (16,500 sq km) and 8% as National Park (9,934 sq km).

People and their homes

- Home ownership in the UK in 2001 was 69.4%, with 9.8% of dwellings privately rented, 6.3% rented from registered social landlords and 14.5% rented from the local authorities. Home ownership increased by 2.5 percentage points in England in the 1990s (to 69.8% in 2001) and 1.5 percentage points in Wales (72.2%), but by 12 percentage points in Scotland (63.1% in 2000).

- Home ownership in the UK (69%) is not especially high. Rates are higher in Ireland (80%), Italy (78%), Spain (78%), Greece (75%), Luxembourg (72%), Australia (71%) and New Zealand (70%), and a little lower in the United States (67%), Portugal (66%) and Belgium (65%). Germany (41%), sometimes quoted as an example for the UK to emulate, has an exceptionally low rate of home ownership.

- However the UK does have an exceptionally small private rented sector by international standards, and an unusually large social rented sector (although the latter has shrunk considerably over the last two decades).

- The UK has the fourth smallest average floor area per dwelling in Europe (79.7 sq m), the second largest average number of rooms per dwelling (5.0) and the second lowest proportion of flats (18%) in the housing stock. So most people live in small houses with exceptionally small rooms.

- Homes are getting smaller. The average size of dwellings built in England from 1980 to 1996 was 10% less than in pre-1980 dwellings. Average plot sizes are also getting smaller.

- The UK has an exceptionally old housing stock compared with other EU countries. In 1991, 48% were pre-1945. Only Belgium had a higher proportion of pre-war stock (50%).

- An estimated 229,000 households in England had a second home in England in 1999/2000, 1.1% of all households. The UK has the second lowest number of

'summer homes' out of the nine European countries for which figures are available.

- Most home moves are over short distances: 20% less than one mile, 57% less than 5 miles and 70% less than 10 miles in England in the three years to 1999/2000.

- Only 8% of population growth in the three southern regions (excluding London) from 1991-98 was caused by net migration from the northern regions and Midlands, and only 12% in London. The largest components of southern population growth are natural growth, net migration out of London and net international migration.

- The above information is from the House Builders' Federation, for further information visit their web site which can be found at www.hbf.co.uk

Shelter applauds government commitment to affordable housing

Shelter strongly welcomes the Government's commitment to increase housing investment by £1.4 billion a year by 2005/6, together with the Chancellor's commitment to tackle homelessness and building new affordable homes. But the charity cautions that the majority of these new resources must be targeted at helping those at the sharp end of the problem – the record 81,000 homeless people and families who are living in the misery of temporary accommodation.

Shelter also welcomes the link between housing and planning at a regional level, which should ensure that, where they are needed, affordable homes are provided as part of all new housing developments. This will help bring the benefits of new developments to local communities. In addition, the announcement to create a single housing inspectorate signals a commitment to more rigorous and consistent standards in social housing, as a way to guarantee that the additional investment announced today benefits those with the greatest housing need.

Ben Jackson, Shelter's Director of External Affairs, commented: 'This is a considerable financial investment from Government, signalling a firm commitment to funding affordable housing. We are delighted to welcome this announcement, but it is crucial this money is targeted at those suffering the misery of homelessness, if it is to help those most in need.'

This significant financial pledge demonstrates a decisive shift from Government following years of underinvestment in affordable housing and campaigning for such measures by Shelter. Shelter estimates that 90,000 affordable homes need to be built each year in order to address this backlog.

- The above information is from Shelter's web site which can be found at www.shelter.org.uk

Affordable housing

Communities plan addresses need for affordable housing in rural areas

Today's commitment to increase the supply of affordable housing in rural areas in the Government's communities plan, announced by the Deputy Prime Minister, is welcome according to the Countryside Agency, the Government's statutory adviser.

Chairman, Sir Ewen Cameron, said: 'We are aware of the very real and natural concerns about the impact of new developments on the countryside. Many feel our countryside capital is being eroded by society's demand for more and more housing. But people need somewhere to live. We welcome the communities plan's call for quality development and the importance of enhancing the living environment. The countryside cannot remain unchanged. In most rural areas – in the north as well as the south – the need for affordable housing is acute and is affecting the viability of many rural communities.

'At the same time, nobody wants to see urban sprawl. We need the right development in the right place – good quality development which enhances our environment and contributes to improving the quality of life in the countryside around towns – including the green belt. With positive management, environmental improvements and proper maintenance of areas of public access and greenways, it can be achieved. We welcome the plan's commitment to provide new country parks and green spaces within towns and encouragement to local partners to replicate the success of the 12 community forests. The Countryside Agency has particular experience in delivering these,' said Sir Ewen.

'New developments must provide:
- opportunities for communities to be involved in the planning and future development of their area
- a range of well-designed housing, including affordable housing
- adequate service provision, such as transport, education and medical facilities, and shops
- open spaces, and
- access to the countryside through planned links between urban and rural areas.'

Sir Ewen Cameron continued: 'Particularly welcome in the communities plan is the requirement for each region to ensure that their strategic approach to investment is "rural proofed" to ensure the sustainability of rural communities; and the modest increase in the Housing Corporation's rural programme to provide 3,500 affordable homes over the period 2004-2006.

> **In most rural areas – in the north as well as the south – the need for affordable housing is acute and is affecting the viability of many rural communities**

'However,' concluded Sir Ewen, 'there is still much to be done. The Government must act quickly on updating planning guidance so that local planning authorities can allocate sites in rural areas for a range of affordable housing.

'We look forward to working with the Government through:
- demonstrating how to deliver quality development in the urban fringe through our work on community engagement, quality of life, concept statements and planning obligations
- providing access to open space and the countryside for people who live in urban areas through our work on Greenways, Doorstep Greens and Community Forests
- better delivery of affordable housing in rural areas through our work on alternative planning policies, sub-regional housing strategies and through our rural housing enablers operating in each county
- and, with the Commission for Architecture and the Built Environment, to take steps to improve the quality of new developments in sensitive rural environments, particularly village extension schemes.'

© Countryside Agency, February 2003

More than just a gateway?

A vision for the rural urban fringe

Hundreds of acres of land between the countryside and towns are underused and overlooked, according to the Countryside Agency and Groundwork. Around each urban area there is a hinterland comprising up to 20% of our total land area that should be a place for our children to play in, a place to improve our health, grow local food and provide sustainable jobs.

We need politicians, local communities, planners and businesses to grab the opportunity to create a vision for the future of the rural/urban fringe and today (Wednesday 28 January) we are launching a consultation on that vision for the land and countryside immediately around towns.

Pam Warhurst, deputy chairman of the Countryside Agency, said: 'It is a common misconception that there is a clear distinction between the countryside – green fields, hedgerows, hills and woodlands – and towns and cities. In reality the two often blur around the edges in a distinctive zone of horse-pastures, public utilities such as electrical substations and struggling agriculture.

'This consultation gives us an opportunity to consider what the rural/urban fringe could mean to the people who live, work and visit there, and how to achieve the best social, economic and environmental benefits from this often overlooked resource.'

Rural Affairs Minister Alun Michael welcomed the vision document: 'The countryside around our towns is not only an important environment for today's generation, but can be a rich asset for our children if we get the planning right. The Rural White Paper set out a vision for the countryside, more diversified since the downturn in agriculture, but bringing landowners and managers closer to the consumers and users of the countryside. A vision for the rural/urban fringe takes this a step further and provides opportunities for farmers to take advantage of the market for local foods, leisure and environmental services.'

Tony Hawkhead, chief executive of Groundwork, said: 'One of the greatest challenges we face as a nation is learning to live more sustainably. This means ensuring that our urban centres develop in harmony with the environment that surrounds them. The rural/urban fringe has enormous potential to help us meet the needs of the present – for local food, recreation, renewable energy and education – while changing the way we live in the future. It is also the bridge that connects our towns and cities with the countryside we love. Groundwork has been helping regenerate the rural/urban fringe for more than 21 years. Now is the time for us to work together to unlock the full potential of this valuable resource.'

Responses to this consultation will help shape a final version of the vision to be launched in mid 2004, followed by further work to stimulate the changes necessary to make the vision a reality.

What is Groundwork?

Groundwork is a federation of Trusts in England, Wales and Northern Ireland, each working with their partners in poor areas to improve the quality of the local environment, the lives of local people and the success of local businesses.

Each Groundwork Trust is a partnership between the public, private and voluntary sectors with its own board of trustees. The work of the Trusts is supported by the national and regional offices of Groundwork UK and by Groundwork Wales.

We work closely with the Government and devolved assemblies, local authorities, regional development agencies and businesses. We also receive support from the European Union, the National Lottery, the landfill tax credit scheme, private sponsors and charitable foundations.

The first Groundwork Trust was established on Merseyside in 1981. There are now nearly 50 Trusts in the UK and a number of Groundwork projects in Eastern Europe. The Groundwork approach has also been adopted in Japan and the USA where the National Park Service is supporting a growing number of Trusts.

Our purpose

Groundwork's purpose is 'to build sustainable communities through joint environmental action'.

We do this by getting residents, businesses and other local organisations involved in practical projects that improve the quality of life, bring about regeneration and lay the foundations for sustainable development.

We believe a 'sustainable community' is one which is vibrant, healthy and safe, which respects the local and global environment and where individuals and enterprise prosper.

For more information on what's happening in your area, contact your local Trust. Visit www.groundwork.org.uk for further information.

© Groundwork

Building more houses 'could benefit wildlife'

By Roger Highfield and David Derbyshire

Building thousands of new homes in the South-East would be good for the environment and could halt the decline in butterflies, birds and other threatened wildlife, an English Nature expert said 9 September 2003.

But rather than concreting over the countryside and creating estates of matchbox homes, new rural housing should have large gardens, plenty of green open spaces and wildlife corridors.

The proposals represent a major change of heart for English Nature, the Government's adviser on nature conservation, which has often been perceived as an obstruction to rural development.

Dr Keith Porter, the agency's environmental information manager, said it was time to shake up the way the countryside was managed and challenge the dominance of food production.

Although farming accounted for 75 per cent of land use in England, it contributed just one per cent to the gross domestic product, he told the conference. Much of the land earmarked for farming after the last war was no longer needed.

'We have got to challenge the dominance of production-driven agriculture,' he said. 'And we have to recognise that there are a lot of uses of the countryside that are currently being pushed out because of the post-war policies of food production.

'We also need to change the perception of wildlife to become a positive contribution to the future of the countryside, not a constraint on development and production.'

That meant having an open mind about new housing and the use of the countryside for tourism and recreation. It also meant linking the income from tourism to the work done by farmers in maintaining rural Britain.

Low-density housing, with large gardens, hedgerows, woodland and open spaces would help farmland birds

New housing could be better for wildlife than arable farms, said Dr Porter.

'The example would be the Deputy Prime Minister's announcement of an increase in housing provision in the South-East. The first thing you see on the news is an environmentalist standing in front of a piece of countryside saying we can't concrete it over.

'When you actually look, what they are standing in front of is wall-to-wall arable – intensive farmland with virtually no wildlife to speak of.'

Low-density housing, with large gardens, hedgerows, woodland and open spaces would help farmland birds, such as song thrushes and skylarks, and butterflies.

'If we get this right, it's not just biodiversity that benefits, it's people that benefit. They can have larger gardens and more attractive surroundings. They will be less stressed because of the better environment around them,' said Dr Porter.

'Emotive comments about concreting over the countryside and destroying our natural environment cannot apply to all the areas being considered. In many areas identified for housing, intensive agriculture dominates the landscapes – the wildlife interest has already been degraded.'

In February the Government earmarked four regions of the South-East for 200,000 new homes: Ashford in Kent, Milton Keynes, Thames Gateway and the M11 corridor.

Brownfield building

Time for the Government to raise its sights on brownfield building

'Good news for the countryside, but the Government must raise its brownfield housing target[1] if the momentum is to be sustained.'

This was the immediate reaction of countryside campaigners CPRE[2] to the news 29 May 2003 that the proportion of new housing built using brownfield sites has continued to increase.[3] The provisional figure for 2002 is 64%.[4]

Henry Oliver, CPRE's Head of Planning, commented:

'Criticism of the Government's 60% brownfield housing target as too low is vindicated by these new figures. We believe the Government should raise its sights higher, to aim for at least 75% of new housing on previously developed land.

'By sticking to its 60% target, the Government risks slowing further progress and sacrificing countryside to unnecessary greenfield development.'

The latest figures also show that the density of new housing has increased, but is still well below the minimum range of 30-50 dwellings per hectare set out in Government planning guidance.[5] CPRE is urging the Government to extend the Density Direction[6] to cover the whole of England without delay.

Henry Oliver concluded: 'Despite good progress, these figures show we are still wasting land by building at very low densities.[7] Government claims that the 60% target is being met largely because of low overall housebuilding rates[8] are missing the point. If last year's housing had been built at 30 dwellings to a hectare, we would have 11% more houses today. At 50 to a hectare we'd have 85% more houses – and all without encroaching on a single extra scrap of land.[9]

'The Government should seize this opportunity to raise its brownfield target and secure better use of scarce land across the country.'

Campaign to Protect Rural England

Notes

1. The Government's target for 60% of new housing to use previously developed urban land and buildings by 2008 was set out in the White Paper *Planning for the Communities of the Future* in February 1998. The target was exceeded in 2000/2001.

2. CPRE exists to promote the beauty, tranquillity and diversity of rural England by encouraging the sustainable use of land and other natural resources in town and country. We promote positive solutions for the long-term future of the countryside and to ensure change values its natural and built environment. Our Patron is Her Majesty The Queen. We have 59,000 supporters, a branch in every county, eight regional groups, over 200 local groups and a national office in central London. CPRE is a powerful combination of effective local action and strong national campaigning. Our President is Sir Max Hastings.

3. *Land Use Change in England*, LUCS-18 May 2003, published by the Office of the Deputy Prime Minister. For further details, see www.planning.odpm.gov.uk/lucs18/01.htm

4. The new figures show that 64% of new housing (including conversions) was built on previously developed land during 2002. This is an increase in the announced figure of 61% in 2001 (subsequently revised to 63%).

5. Planning Policy Guidance note (PPG) 3 *Housing* (March 2000).

6. ODPM Circular 01/02 *The Town and Country Planning (Residential Density) (London and South East England) Direction 2002* requires local planning authorities to notify the Secretary of State of any application for housing development which they intend to permit and which: is on a site of one hectare or more or sets the context for development of a larger area than that in the application; and proposes a density of lower than 30 dwellings per hectare. The Direction applies, however, only to London and the South East (including Essex, Bedfordshire and Buckinghamshire).

7. The data show that the average density for all new housing is still only 27 dwellings per hectare, well below the 30 dpha minimum in PPG3 (see note 5). On greenfield sites, the figure is significantly lower, at 23 dpha.

8. 'While I am pleased to see we are exceeding our target for building new housing on brownfield land, I am concerned this is being achieved at a time of record lows in housebuilding.' The Rt Hon. Lord Rooker, Minister for Housing, Planning and Regeneration, quoted in an ODPM Press Release, 29 May 2003.

9. 30-27=3; 3/27x100=11%. 50-27=23; 23/27x100=85%.

■ The Campaign to Protect Rural England (CPRE) exists to promote the beauty, tranquillity and diversity of rural England by encouraging the sustainable use of land and other natural resources in town and country.

■ The above information is from CPRE's web site which can be found at www.cpre.org.uk

© Campaign to Protect Rural England (CPRE)

> *'By sticking to its 60% target, the Government risks slowing further progress and sacrificing countryside to unnecessary greenfield development'*

Builders 'have enough land for 280,000 houses'

House builders have enough land with planning permission for more than a quarter of a million new homes, conservationists claim

A survey by the Campaign to Protect Rural England (CPRE) suggests that the top construction companies' land reserves have expanded by almost 18 per cent in the past five years.

It called on the Government to give more support to urban renewal rather than greenfield development and said more money was needed to provide affordable homes for the poorly paid.

'These results show what we have long suspected; that the house builders' special pleading for more greenfield land to build on is not borne out by the facts,' said Neil Sinden, director of policy.

'Far from there being a land shortage, too much countryside is still in the pipeline for development. Instead of allowing the designation of more greenfield land, urgent action is needed to boost the attractiveness of urban renewal instead.'

The survey claims that the leading house builders possess sufficient land with at least outline planning permission to build 278,866 homes – enough for a row of terrace houses stretching from Land's End to John o'Groats.

By Graham Tibbetts

Although the number of completed new dwellings increased by seven per cent last year, this was outstripped by the increase in the size of 'landbanks'.

The CPRE criticised 'excessive greenfield housing allocations'. It demanded that the Government introduce further tax breaks and financial incentives to favour urban regeneration over greenfield encroachment.

The CPRE also recommended that the target for putting new housing on brownfield sites should be increased from 60 per cent to at least 75 per cent.

The leading house builders possess sufficient land with at least outline planning permission to build 278,866 homes

In addition to the call for more affordable housing, it also said the Government should tackle the problems of regional disparities in prosperity and reduce development in overheated areas.

The survey was heavily criticised by the House Builders' Federation.

A spokesman said: 'One wonders why an organisation that champions "nimbyism" is accusing house builders of failing to build sufficient homes.

'You would think they would be pleased. The reality is it's trying to knock an industry that is effectively fighting back by demonstrating Britain's acute housing shortage and the damage this is doing socially and economically.

'These figures do not tie up with other surveys and completely miss the point of whether these sites are viable for development.'

He said that local authorities often demanded an expensive 'shopping list' of libraries, theatres, cinemas and swimming pools as a price for planning permission, rendering many proposed developments financially unviable.

© Telegraph Group Limited, London 2004

Building for life

Information from Building for Life – a partnership between the House Builders' Federation, CABE and the Civic Trust

Building for Life is a commitment to the quality of new homes made by three partners:

- the house-building industry, represented by the House Builders' Federation
- the government, represented by the Commission for Architecture and the Built Environment (CABE)
- the campaigners, represented by the Civic Trust

Over the next three years Building for Life will do three things:

- we will identify great new housing schemes, both at home and abroad, and explain to the house-building industry why these designs work so well and how they can learn from them
- we will seek to understand better the aspirations of people buying homes so that the design of new housing is more attractive to them
- we will identify the barriers to designing quality new homes and we will campaign to remove them

When we buy a home we make important personal choices:

- is this a home that is built well, that will be easy to maintain and which will change and adapt to meet my changing personal circumstances; will it minimise its impact on the environment and keep my energy bills low at the same time?
- is this a neighbourhood where I can catch a bus into town and walk to local shops, where my children can play safely and where I have easy access to the pub, the sports centre and other facilities?
- is this a place that I am proud to live, a place of character and distinction, that lifts my spirits when I turn the corner into my street and when I open my front door?

Too many homes built in the last 30 years have failed these crucial tests. But times change.

The country needs a vibrant and healthy house-building industry to contribute to our national economy.

> *There are signs that things are getting better. There are now house builders, both large and small, building homes and places that are functional, attractive and desirable*

There is a social imperative. If government predictions are right, we will have to accommodate an additional 3.8 million new homes in the next 25 years. Many of these new homes will have to be developed in difficult urban locations.

At the same time, our housing stock is now the oldest in Europe. While some of these older properties have stood the test of time, others are no longer desirable and are being abandoned. There is an urgent need for renewal.

There are signs that things are getting better. There are now house builders, both large and small, building homes and places that are functional, attractive and desirable. While we know there is no room for complacency – there are still dreadful houses being built – we can recognise and celebrate examples of considerable design achievement.

We will celebrate the best so that we can raise the standards of the rest.

- The above information is from Building for Life. If you have any comments or questions about Building for Life, please contact them at enquiries@buildingforlife.org or visit their web site which can be found at www.buildingforlife.org/homepage.html

© 2004 Building for Life – a partnership between the House Builders' Federation, CABE and the Civic Trust

One million sustainable homes

Information from WWF-UK

WWF's One Million Sustainable Homes campaign aims to tackle the harmful effect that our houses have on the environment. The goal is to provide people with the choice of living in a home that is healthier, safer and cheaper for them and the environment.

WWF is calling on the British government and the regional assemblies to commit themselves to developing a million sustainable homes by 2012 (including new build and refurbishment of existing houses).

WWF launched its groundbreaking campaign One Million Sustainable Homes in August 2002, at the World Summit on Sustainable Development in Johannesburg.

Why sustainable homes?

If everyone on the planet were to consume natural resources and pollute the environment as we currently do in the UK, we would need three planets to support us!

The majority of existing UK housing stock has significant social and environmental impacts. For example, in typical new built homes in the UK, total energy use is three-and-a-half-times more than in Denmark and Germany. In social terms, this clearly has consequences for people who have difficulty in affording to heat their homes properly. According to the Joseph Rowntree Foundation:

'Britain has around 40,000 more deaths during December and March than expected from death rates in other months of the year, which is a larger "winter excess" than in most other European countries, including Scandinavia. This is in spite of the fact that Britain has comparatively mild winters... part of the explanation may lie with Britain's ageing housing stock, which . . . may provide less protection against the cold.'

In environmental terms, the residential sector in the UK contributes around 27 per cent of the total CO_2 emissions associated with energy use, and domestic energy use is projected to rise by six per cent by 2010. It is therefore essential to reduce emissions from existing houses and from new homes.

Furthermore, up to 70 per cent of all timber consumed in the UK goes into the construction industry, and much of this wood comes from forests around the world that are not managed in a sustainable way.

Other significant impacts related to the construction/refurbishment of houses include:

- the widespread use of toxic chemicals in building materials, which can pose significant risks to the occupants and the wider environment;
- quarrying to provide basic raw construction materials like aggregates; and
- the inefficient use of water in houses that are not designed with water efficiency in mind.

'Countryside Properties is very pleased to support WWF's campaign for One Million Sustainable Homes in the UK by 2012. Countryside commits to build all new houses to a minimum standard of EcoHomes "Good", with increasing numbers of developments achieving standards of "Very Good" and "Excellent" over the next ten years. We look forward to contributing to the campaign to make sustainable homes a mainstream reality throughout the UK.'
Alan Cherry MBE, Chairman, Countryside Properties PLC

'The House Builders' Federation is delighted to support the One Million Sustainable Homes initiative and looks forward to exploring ways in which it can be involved in promoting its aims with members.'
Robert Ashmead, Chief Executive, House Builders' Federation

'We are pleased to support the WWF campaign. CIRIA looks forward to contributing to the development, dissemination and adoption of best practice to help convert these aspirations into reality.'
Dr Peter Bansby, Director General, Construction Industry Research and Information Association

- The above information is from WWF UK's web site which can be found at www.wwf.org.uk
© *WWF-UK*

On the home front

Improving the housing environment and delivering 'sustainable communities'

Another housing crisis?

There has seldom been a time when more effort and money have been expended in calculating the exact extent of the UK's housing problems. Although figures are often disputed a number of trends have received universal acceptance.

There are too many poor-quality homes. Large amounts of housing stock do not reach the decent homes standard, with significant consequences for health, well-being and the environment.

There are not enough homes where people want them. The trend towards longer and more dispersed living and the emergence of economic 'hot spots', especially in London and the South East, is exacerbating housing shortages and threatening quality of life.

There are too many housing areas sliding into decline. Many traditional housing areas are suffering 'neighbourhood collapse' due to economic decline and outward migration.

These trends are set against a backdrop of radical changes in housing tenure, particularly in relation to social housing which is subject to right-to-buy legislation and housing-stock transfers. These changes demand a new set of relationships to ensure that housing providers remain accountable and residents continue to have a say in decisions that affect them.

The new challenges

What makes this housing crisis different from those of previous generations is that public policy-makers have realised that housing problems cannot be addressed in isolation from wider issues of neighbourhood quality and social cohesion.

The importance of creating and maintaining high quality public open spaces and more 'liveable' communities has risen to the top of the political agenda.

By Graham Duxbury

ODPM's Sustainable Communities programme makes this link between housing, public space and environmental quality explicit, promising a 'joined up' approach to housing and regeneration within a framework of regional development.

It also throws up three fundamental challenges which must be addressed:

Reversing the decline in 'traditional' housing areas – in the short term 'managing decline' but in the longer term finding strategies for housing market renewal which energise and empower residents and create the conditions within which damaged communities can recover.

Managing growth and quality of life – safeguarding environmental quality in high-density areas by building open-space networks into growth areas and creating a new stimulus for people-friendly and ecologically-friendly design.

Establishing a new neighbourliness – not turning the clock back to a 'golden age' of good neighbourliness but building new local connections and rediscovering the importance of 'place' in an increasingly fragmented society.

Groundwork and the housing environment

Groundwork has more than 20 years' experience of working with residents to improve 'community spaces' on their doorstep and offers a partnership-based and bottom-up mechanism for delivering public policy objectives at neighbourhood level.

Groundwork is currently working with more than 70 registered social landlords to improve housing areas. These partnerships have the potential to deliver significant activity in five key areas:

- improving housing-related environments
- engaging residents in local decision-making
- addressing crime and the fear of crime
- delivering local learning, skills and jobs
- developing strategic approaches to open space.

Based on its experience, Groundwork believes the following measures would contribute to achieving a more integrated approach to housing and liveability policy while enabling more effective partnership working and delivery at local level.

Regional housing boards should be directed to include plans to improve liveability in regional housing strategies.

Regional housing strategies should be developed alongside regional green-space strategies, both within the framework of long-term sustainable development.

Housing market renewal pathfinders should develop strategic working relationships with environmental regeneration agencies.

Learning & Skills Councils, regional development agencies and housing associations should prioritise support for estate-based employment programmes and new social enterprises as a vehicle for improving housing and housing environments.

Greater use should be made of voluntary sector intermediary organisations to help residents play a more active role in local decision-making and long-term management strategies.

The Thames Gateway cabinet committee should underline the importance of green-space networks as an essential component of growth strategies.

- The above information is from Groundwork's web site which can be found at www.groundwork.org.uk Alternatively see their address details on page 41.

© Groundwork

The Communities Plan

Sustainable communities overview

The Deputy Prime Minister launched the Communities Plan (Sustainable Communities: Building for the future) on 5 February 2003. The Plan sets out a long-term programme of action for delivering sustainable communities in both urban and rural areas. It aims to tackle housing supply issues in the South East, low demand in other parts of the country, and the quality of our public spaces. The Plan includes not just a significant increase in resources and major reforms of housing and planning, but a new approach to how we build and what we build.

This £22 billion programme of action aims to focus the attention and co-ordinate the efforts of all levels of Government and stakeholders in bringing about development that meets the economic, social and environmental needs of future generations as well as succeeding now.

Key themes

The Plan consists of several key elements:

- Addressing the housing shortage, which comprises:

1. Accelerating the provision of housing. This includes: ensuring that housing numbers set out in planning guidance for the South East (RPG 9) are delivered; accelerating growth in the four 'growth areas' (Thames Gateway, London-Stansted-Cambridge corridor, Ashford, and Milton Keynes-South Midlands); and ensuring that the construction industry has the right skills to deliver.

2. Affordable housing. £5 billion has been allocated for the provision of affordable housing over the next three years. This includes £1 billion for housing 'key workers' in the public sector, to aid recruitment and retention.

3. Tackling homelessness. Including ensuring ending the use of bed-and-breakfast hostels for homeless families by March 2004.

Programme funding

The Government is investing £22 billion over 2002/3 to 2005/6 to improve housing and communities. Key funding initiatives include:

- An extra £201 million to improve parks and public spaces.
- Investing £350 million to speed up and modernise the planning system.
- Investing £5 billion over the next three years to regenerate deprived areas.
- £610 million for the growth areas.
- £500 million to tackle low demand and abandonment issues.
- £2.8 billion to bring council homes up to a decent standard.

Source: ODPM

- Addressing low demand and abandonment. Around one million homes in parts of the North and Midlands are suffering from low demand and abandonment. Nine pathfinder schemes have been established in the areas worst affected to put in place action programmes to turn this problem around.

- Decent homes. The Plan sets out an action programme to ensure that all social housing is brought up to a decent standard by 2010, alongside targeted action to improve conditions for vulnerable people in private housing.

- Liveability. The Plan sets out how the Government intends to intensify efforts to improve the local environment of all communities. This includes cleaner streets, improved parks and better public spaces.

- Protecting the countryside. The Plan outlines how land will be used more effectively. The majority of new housing will be on previously developed land, rather than on greenfield. The area of land designated as green-belt land will be increased or maintained in each area. Developments not meeting density standards in the South East will be called in.

Source: Office of the Deputy Prime Minister (ODPM), © Crown copyright

KEY FACTS

- There is a serious shortage of homes across the whole of southern and eastern England. (p. 1)

- Currently, the number of people coming to live in Britain is greater than the number of people leaving. (p. 2)

- House prices are now so high that it is possible for a household with an income of £25,000 a year to buy a home in only ten out 212 local authority districts in the whole of southern England. (p. 2)

- In the first 11 months of 2003, the number of first-time buyers slumped to the lowest level on record, 330,540. (p. 6)

- The Halifax said prices in the North were up 33.7 per cent in a year to an average of £103,314. This takes the increase over two years to 60 per cent. (p. 6)

- Single people have become the driving force behind the housing market in London where, in 2002, they made up over 50 per cent of buyers. (p. 7)

- Single people make up 27 per cent of UK households, up from 18 per cent 30 years ago, but account for 40 per cent of mortgage borrowing. (p. 7)

- By 2010, single-person households will predominate, accounting for almost 40 per cent of all households in the UK. (p. 7)

- It is accepted that up to 40 per cent of new homes will have to be built on greenfield land. (p. 9)

- The average cost of buying a home in London is £228,625 compared to a national average of £140,624. (p. 10)

- To buy an average-priced home in London would require a single gross salary of over £62,055. The average annual London salary is £32,448. (p. 10)

- Plans to build half a million homes between the Wash and the Thames by 2021 were approved yesterday by the eastern regional assembly despite Essex and Hertfordshire councils' belief that the counties could not cope with the additions. (p. 18)

- Britain will need a new city the size of Leeds to be built over the next decade if it is to tackle the chronic housing shortage which leads to rocketing house prices that keep potential first-time buyers off the property ladder. (p. 20)

- The crisis is affecting the poorest parts of the country. The number of households in England which have been classed as homeless this year is set to top 200,000 for the first time in a decade. (p. 20)

- Before 2016 it is predicted that England alone will have to accommodate an additional 4.4 million households. (p. 25)

- There are 997,000 empty homes in the UK, 4.1% of the stock. Government-owned stock is 16% vacant. 6% of properties in London are empty. (p. 25)

- In 1981 there were approximately 4% more dwellings than households in England, just sufficient to provide a home for every household and leave a margin for vacant dwellings. But in the last 20 years household growth has far exceeded expansion of the housing stock. (p. 29)

- Home ownership in the UK in 2001 was 69.4%, with 9.8% of dwellings privately rented, 6.3% rented from registered social landlords and 14.5% rented from the local authorities. (p. 30)

- Home ownership in the UK (69%) is not especially high. Rates are higher in Ireland (80%), Italy (78%), Spain (78%), Greece (75%), Luxembourg (72%), Australia (71%) and New Zealand (70%), and a little lower in the United States (67%), Portugal (66%) and Belgium (65%). (p. 30)

- Homes are getting smaller. The average size of dwellings built in England from 1980 to 1996 was 10% less than in pre-1980 dwellings. Average plot sizes are also getting smaller. (p. 30)

- Although farming accounted for 75 per cent of land use in England, it contributed just one per cent to the gross domestic product. (p. 33)

- The leading house builders possess sufficient land with at least outline planning permission to build 278,866 homes – enough for a row of terrace houses stretching from Land's End to John o'Groats. (p. 35)

- The CPRE also recommended that the target for putting new housing on brownfield sites should be increased from 60 per cent to at least 75 per cent. (p. 35)

- WWF is calling on the British government and the regional assemblies to commit themselves to developing a million sustainable homes by 2012. (p. 37)

- Furthermore, up to 70 per cent of all timber consumed in the UK goes into the construction industry, and much of this wood comes from forests around the world that are not managed in a sustainable way. (p. 37)

ADDITIONAL RESOURCES

You might like to contact the following organisations for further information. Due to the increasing cost of postage, many organisations cannot respond to enquiries unless they receive a stamped, addressed envelope.

Campaign to Protect Rural England (CPRE)
128 Southwark Street
London, SE1 0SW
Tel: 020 7981 2800
Fax: 020 7981 2899
E-mail: info@cpre.org.uk
Web site: www.cpre.org.uk
CPRE exists to promote the beauty, tranquillity and diversity of rural England by encouraging the sustainable use of land and other natural resources in town and country.

Country Land and Business Association
16 Belgrave Square
London, SW1X 8PQ
Tel: 020 7235 0511
Fax: 020 7235 4696
E-mail: mail@cla.org.uk
Web site: www.cla.org.uk
The CLA was founded almost one hundred years ago to protect the interests of owners of rural land in England and Wales.

Friends of the Earth (FOE)
26-28 Underwood Street
London, N1 7JQ
Tel: 020 7490 1555
Fax: 020 7490 0881
E-mail: info@foe.co.uk
Web site: www.foe.co.uk
As an independent environmental group, Friends of the Earth publishes a comprehensive range of leaflets, books and in-depth briefings and reports.

Groundwork
85-87 Cornwall Street
Birmingham, B3 3BY
Tel: 0121 236 8565
Fax: 0121 236 7356
E-mail: info@groundwork.org.uk
Web site: www.groundwork.org.uk
Groundwork is a leading environmental regeneration charity making sustainable development a reality in many of the UK's most disadvantaged communities.

House Builders' Federation
56-64 Leonard Street
London, EC2A 4JX
Tel: 020 7608 5100
Fax: 020 7608 5101
E-mail: hbf@hbf.co.uk
Web site: www.hbf.c1o.uk
The House Builders' Federation is the voice of the housebuilding industry in England and Wales.

Joseph Rowntree Foundation (JRF)
The Homestead
40 Water End
York, YO30 6WP
Tel: 01904 629241
Fax: 01904 620072
E-mail: infor@jrf.org.uk
Web site: www.jrf.org.uk
The Foundation is an independent, non-political body which funds programmes of research and innovative development in the fields of housing, social care and social policy. It publishes its research findings rapidly and widely so that they can inform current debate and practice.

London Housing Federation
175 Gray's Inn Road
London, WC1X 8UP
Tel: 020 7278 6571
Fax: 020 7837 7473
E-mail: london@housing.org.uk
Web site: www.housing.org.uk
The National Housing Federation is the body that represents the independent social housing sector. They have around 1400 non-profit housing organisations currently in membership and the number is growing all the time. Between them they own or manage around 1.8 million homes.

London Wildlife Trust (LWT)
Harling House
47-51 Great Suffolk Street
London, SE1 0BS
Tel: 020 7261 0447
Fax: 020 7261 0538

E-mail: enquiries@londonwt.cix.co.uk
Web site: www.wildlondon.org.uk
Promotes nature conservation within Greater London and encourages a greater public awareness of the value of wildlife in and beyond the urban setting.

Shelter
88 Old Street
London, EC1V 9HU
Tel: 020 7505 2000
Fax: 020 7505 2169
E-mail: info@shelter.org.uk
Web site: www.shelter.org.uk
Campaigns for decent homes that everyone can afford. Produces publications.

Town and Country Planning Association
17 Carlton House Terrace
London, SW1Y 5AS
Tel: 020 7930 8903
Fax: 020 7930 3280
E-mail: tcpa@tcpa.org.uk
Web site: www.tcpa.org.uk
The charitable purpose of the Town and Country Planning Association is to improve the art and science of town and country planning. It is the only independent organisation for planning and housing covering the UK and the longest-established planning body in the world.

WWF-UK
Panda House
Weyside Park
Catteshall Lane
Godalming, GU7 1XR
Tel: 01483 426444
Fax: 01483 426409
Web site: www.wwf.org.uk
WWF-UK is the British arm of the largest independent international conservation organisation in the world. WWF works with government, industry, media and the public to protect the decline in animal and plant species and reduce pollution.

INDEX

ACKNOWLEDGEMENTS

The publisher is grateful for permission to reproduce the following material.

While every care has been taken to trace and acknowledge copyright, the publisher tenders its apology for any accidental infringement or where copyright has proved untraceable. The publisher would be pleased to come to a suitable arrangement in any such case with the rightful owner.

Chapter One: Housing Problems

Home truths, © Town and Country Planning Association, *Homes*, © Town and Country Planning Association, *Where the housing ladder is out of reach*, © Guardian Newspapers Limited 2004, *Highest house prices*, © Joseph Rowntree Foundation, *Government 'failing rural poor' on housing*, © Guardian Newspapers Limited 2004, *Property boom squeezes out the first-time buyers*, © The Daily Mail, January 2004, *House price rises 2003*, © The Daily Mail, January 2004, *Singles now major players in housing market*, © Estate Agency News, *The crisis of affordable housing*, © Town and Country Planning Association, *Incomes required to access home-ownership*, © Town and Country Planning Association, *The growing use of temporary accommodation*, © Town and Country Planning Association, *Tipping the balance*, © London Housing Federation, *The cost of buying in the private sector*, © London Housing Federation, *London's housing crisis*, © Greater London Authority 2004, *Housing and the environment*, © Crown copyright is reproduced with the permission of Her Majesty's Stationery Office, *Environmental issues*, © Crown copyright is reproduced with the permission of Her Majesty's Stationery Office, *Brownfield? Greenfield?*, © London Wildlife Trust, *500,000 new homes for M11 region*, © Guardian Newspapers Limited 2004, *Building problems for the future*, © Guardian Newspapers Limited 2004, *Wanted: new city to solve UK housing crisis*, © Guardian Newspapers Limited 2004, *Household growth in England*, © Crown copyright is reproduced with the permission of Her Majesty's Stationery Office.

Chapter Two: Housing Solutions

Have I got the house for you, © Guardian Newspapers Limited 2004, *120,000 new homes on the way*, © Telegraph Group Limited, London 2004, *Urban land in Britain*, © Friends of the Earth, *Measures to increase housing stock*, © Friends of the Earth, *Communities not concrete*, © Campaign to Protect Rural England (CPRE), *Major growth*, © Crown copyright is reproduced with the permission of Her Majesty's Stationery Office, *The rural housing crisis*, © 2004 Country Land & Business Association, *The unaffordable cost of affordable housing*, © House Builders' Federation, *Shelter applauds government commitment to affordable housing*, © Shelter, *Affordable housing*, © Countryside Agency, *More than just a gateway?*, © Groundwork, *Building more houses 'could benefit wildlife'*, © Telegraph Group Limited, London 2004, *Brownfield building*, © Campaign to Protect Rural England (CPRE), *Builders 'have enough land for 280,000 houses'*, © Telegraph Group Limited, London 2004, *Building for life*, © 2004 Building for Life, *One million sustainable homes*, © WWF-UK, *On the home front*, © Groundwork, *The Communities Plan*, © Crown copyright is reproduced with the permission of Her Majesty's Stationery Office.

Photographs and illustrations:

Pages 1, 7, 19, 28, 35, 39: Simon Kneebone; pages 5, 21, 36: Bev Aisbett; pages 13, 31: Pumpkin House; page 15: Angelo Madrid; page 16: Miranda Waugh; page 33: Don Hatcher.

Craig Donnellan
Cambridge
April, 2004